The White Queen

Gambhir Watts

ISBN: 978-1-950088-31-7

Dedication

I dedicate this book to my late parents:

Ranjit Kaur Babbr Watts (mother) and

Dr Sukhdev Watts (father)

Acknowledgment

I record my acknowledgement to the people, apart from parents, who mattered most to me and influenced chartering my life flow:

Sir Pritamdev Pamnani, my High School teacher who loved me like his child and infused great confidence in me

Mr Chemburkar, my first Supervisor in Bank of India who guided me and looked after me and my welfare like his child

Dr D M Munshi, my college professor who was my guide and inspirer in starting for my own consultancy practice

Mr Prem Kumar Khurana, one of my first major client who helped me with my own office premises in the heart of Posh business district Nariman Point, Bombay

Mr Prem Kumar Gupta my first client from a major business house of India who became my long time close friend and well-wisher and promoted my consultancy services to friends and extended family

My children Moksha and Govinda who constantly

inspired me to overcome any adversity and I learned a lot from them

And three ladies in my life who taught me hard lessons: Meera Chaudhary, my first girl friend from high school; Durga Rupani, my girl friend from Bank of India who loved me most but had to ditch me and finally Bhoji my wife for being my constant critic and teaching me a lesson of my life

About the Author

Gambhir Watts is multitasking Professional with over 35 years Executive experienced in not-for-profit organisations, business/financial/project management, strategic planning, business development, turnaround, trouble shooting, start-ups, contract/joint venture negotiation in US / Australia/ India/International arenas.

Awards Conferred for distinguished service to the community on issues involving ethics, values, religion and social change:

- Order of Australia Medal (OAM) conferred on 10 June 2013
- **GOPIO COMMUNITY SERVICE AWARD** In Recognition of Outstanding Community Service To The People Of Australia And India – January 2011
- **INTERNATIONAL SARDAR RATNA AWARD** For Excellence In The Field Of Globalisation Of Sardar's Ideology & Social Development Displaying Benevolent Services Towards Country

& Countrymen – January 2011 by Sardar Patel Foundation

Professional Qualifications and Memberships

- MALP (Master of Administrative Law and Policy, Sydney University)
- FCPA (Fellow of CPA Australia)
- MAICD (Member Australian Institute of Company Directors)
- CTA (Chartered Tax Advisor, The Tax Institute)
- FCMA (Fellow Institute of Costs Accountants of India)
- FAIM (Fellow, Australian Institute of Management)
- FIBM (Fellow, British Institute of Management)
- FSRA – Fellow Royal Society of Arts, UK
- Master Commerce (Bombay University, India)

Preface

Corruption – a scandalous word that elicits the listener's interest the moment it is uttered. Despite how ubiquitous it is in our modern understanding of our world, corruption is still a deeply misunderstood topic. Due to this general ignorance, those who practice it are able to getaway while the rest of us are left trying to grasp what *exactly* corruption is.

What needs to be understood is that corruption is a system – it does not arise out of a vacuum. We all hate it and wish to blame someone or something for causing it, but it isn't always as simple as that. Structural reasons encourage people to indulge in corrupt behavior, which is why corruption takes on so many different forms depending on the location.

We will explore these *"structural reasons"* in this book with the help of my experience in the finance and consultancy sectors, both of which are particularly rife with corruption, in India and Australia. Through this retelling, you will see that no geographic boundaries or cultural phenomenon prevent or encourage corruption. Rather, they only make corruption take on different forms. Corruption itself remains.

Contents

Page Left Blank Intentionally

Chapter 1
My First Exposure to the Adult World

Adults and children live in their divided worlds. Children live in a world where everything seems possible for them. Conversely, adults live in a world where everything seems impossible to them. Children simply live their lives without a care in this world, but the adults make it their mission to bring complications into their life. Is it because children are naïve and unaware of the fact that there is more to life than just eating, napping, and watching cartoons? Children do not have to worry about things like filling up their banks and paying off their bills.

They don't know that to live a comfortable life, they need to be backed up financially. I know that the transition from childhood to adulthood is not smooth. The pubescent years are not easy to deal with, as that is the time when we are discovering more and more about ourselves. The truth is that we keep finding new things about ourselves along the road of life. These discoveries don't merely stop when we reach the age of 20. That's what my life was about. I kept discovering new things about myself, even after living for more than fifty years. As a teenager myself, I did not feel the impending doom like others. I was more than ecstatic to join the world of adults as soon as I could. It was a way for me to help my family out financially. I thought that it was finally time to put myself at use. My father was the sole bread-winner of the family, consisting of nine members. It was not easy to feed nine mouths, but he managed to do it well until he could not afford to do it alone anymore.

He needed help as the world economy kept crashing, and the prices kept going up. I helped him out by wrapping candy in a factory when I was merely ten years of age, and going to a school seemed highly improbable for me. I had to sacrifice my education to help out my father, but I did it anyway. This does not mean that I came from a family with an uneducated background.

My father was very well-educated with a strong command of the English language due to his association with the British army before the partition took place in India. He settled in Mumbai after the partition of India. The area we lived in had many Sindhi medium schools, but unfortunately, none of them offered education in English. Father sent my eldest brother to an English medium school far from our home with high hopes. He wanted his eldest son to could study well and take the mantle from him — a hope that my brother brutally shattered by mingling with the wrong company and ruining himself in the process. This created a massive barrier between me and my desire to receive an education. Many of my father's friends were not literate, but were still well-established people and were wealthy businessmen. Due to some unbeknownst reason, this had planted a seed of doubt over the importance of education in my father's mind.

Couple that with my brother's actions, and the doors to me getting an education were closed shut by my father. He was an educated man, but was not relying on logic when he deemed education to be futile. He wasn't willing to let me attend school at all. All I ever dreamt of was becoming an educated individual. As someone who craved knowledge, this scenario greatly devastated me.

"Why?" I would always ask my father stubbornly, *"Why can't I go to school?"*

He would glare and merely say, *"Because I said so."*

I couldn't understand his aversion to education at all. After all, I expected him to understand my desire since he was from an educated background. Surely, he would know the importance of education despite the circumstances we were living in. I was wrong to expect anything from him, but I didn't give up at the idea of education. Surprisingly, my mother backed me up. My mother supported me even though she herself was not formally educated in English – though, she came from a well-educated family. She was always there by my side during this crusade.

Despite everything that was going on, she stood by me and kept encouraging me to pursue my education. To gain all the knowledge that a school going child does, I went to several tuition centers and even studied at home. I also learned how to read, write, and speak the English language through my father's help. He was willing to teach me the English language, even when he was against sending me to a schooling institute.

The private tuitions and extensive study sessions at home, that went on for a couple of years, allowed me to catch up drastically, and I was able to join school directly in the Eighth Standard. As mine was an unusual case, I was allowed admission in the girl's section. We were only five boys amidst forty odd girls, and this was unchartered territory for me. Throughout the entire process, I was highly encouraged and aided by both, the Principal of the school and the State Inspector General of Schools. This predicament is one of the main reasons behind my shy, reserved nature. In a weird way, it has shaped me to who I am today. I was teased a lot in the past, but it only improved my ability to ignore the noise and disregard any baseless criticism that I came across. I always kept to myself, unlike other guys who fought with each other to get some attention from girls.

However, my behavior resulted in the exact opposite manner I was gaining a lot of unwanted attention by merely being *"the good kid."* I had also won the confidence of my father as he was proud and forgiving when he saw how well I was doing at school and how much the teachers adored me. I had my first, innocent encounter with corruption in this school. I couldn't notice it then, but over time, I realized that even children are subjected to corruption at a young age.

In my opinion, school is where corruption first begins. Nepotism and favoritism are two branches of the corruption tree. Despite being non-monetary, they help in the cultivation of a corrupt environment for the students. It may sound appalling to call favoritism a form of corruption, but many students can agree on how it helped in creating barriers between them. It creates a sense of injustice in the students as they feel as if they are being mistreated. Those students who are underestimated on a daily basis later on develop a form of inferiority complex that affects them outside of school premises. This is a type of corruption that goes under the radar and can lead to incredibly unbelievable acts in the future. At first, it feels excellent being the center of attention of all the teachers since it helps you gain popularity.

However, the same reputation, when targeted at someone else, makes you empathize with those who feel left out and neglected. Despite being non-monetary, this is the worst kind of corruption to take place inside school premises. Being biased toward someone so early on in their lives doesn't only corrupt their minds and character, but also creates a false set of ideas for them to follow.

The 'favorite' students, on the other hand, develop a superiority complex because they feel as if they are entitled to have everything good in life. This creates another set of hindrances for favorite students later in life. Looking at it retrospectively, I realize that corruption had its ugly presence in our school as well. I have always been a follower and believe that it should be avoided as much as possible. During my time as a student in school, a senior teacher who had specialized in Hindi was popularly known as 'Punjabi Sir.' He had a favorite female student named Meera. This teacher would always put her ahead of me by manipulating marks, especially in his subject, Hindi. Coincidentally, Meera and I were close friends since we were both high achievers in our school. We had a friendly competition with each other. Our relationship later on developed from being platonic, and we started dating each other.

Meera had an advantage over me in the Hindi language due to this teacher. Our friendship soon turned sour due to the apparent favoritism displayed by the Punjabi sir regarding her. Unfortunately for me, his bias was not limited to the examinations held at the school. Later on, 'Punjabi Sir' did the same when he was chosen as an examiner for the final Higher Secondary Exams conducted by the State Government. Suspiciously, Meera topped in our school, and I came in second after her with a difference of 30 marks.

I am not saying this as a disgruntled and jealous runner-up – at least, not entirely. This is because the difference in

Hindi, for which this teacher was the examiner, was of 36 marks! Based on my command over the Sanskrit language, and it is one of the roots of Hindi, I doubt that I was that bad at it given how well my exam had gone. This reveals the unfortunate and ugly truth that we have been surrounded by a corrupt environment from a very young age. At one point or another, we all come across a point where we become aware of such corruption taking place. After we finished school, it was around April 1966, and I had just completed my High Secondary Board exams from Netaji High School at the mere age of 16. Meera had left for a different college and started avoiding me. One of the excuses she gave was related to the difference in caste.

She was from a Sindhi family, whereas I was from a Punjabi family. After three years of sharing more than just my friendship, she had suddenly become aware that our families would never agree if our relationship grew out of proportion and she decided to cut all ties with me. She didn't want to do anything with me due to the age-old issue of caste difference.

I guess that was another rite of passage that I had to go through to get to where I am now; as they say, *"The show must go on."* Step by step, I realized that we all have to go different things before we enter into the world of adults. I don't think we all know where we're standing until we go through tough times of our own. It might be a game for 'Punjabi Sir,' who tried to show-off his influence. However, it was a severe matter for me. When you're a student and know that someone else ruined your chances of topping, it feels as if your world has been shattered into shambles. My entire existence at that point depended on my marks because it could help me get into a good college in the future. If the rest of my teachers were like Punjabi Sir, then my future would have been done for. Thanks to the honestly displayed by other teachers, I was able to pull through happily. Another type of corruption that I encountered in my school days was private tuition centers.

A majority of the teachers in school also taught privately in the evening or on weekends. I don't have anything against them as I acquired my primary knowledge from a similar facility. What I can't entirely agree with is the unfair treatment based on who attends their classes. They favored those students who participated in a teacher's private tuition class in school.

They could get away with things an average student could never get away with before. What if someone is a genius, but can barely afford school fees and can't go to the tuition center? Why should someone who understands what's taught in school take additional classes after school or on weekends? Isn't it the school's responsibility to educate all students equally? Does this mean that these teachers don't care about their performance in school? All of these questions highlight the presence of corruption in a school system. Making additional money was not the problem here. Forcing your students to resort to teaching centers due to their pathetic performances in school was the main issue. If you carefully consider the situation, such teachers are just taking extra money from the students and in return, providing them with special treatment.

The more I became aware of these things, the heavier my heart felt. It made me realize that life at school was quite challenging to handle. I understood how easy it was for the students to go astray and finally understood my brother's behavior. It's easy to be manipulated by others in school. You're exposed to a lot of people who come from different backgrounds and carry different values with them. Being shy and introverted helped me greatly. I started analyzing others before taking a step forward to befriend them. This proved to be beneficial for me later in life as I avoided mingling with the wrong people as much as I could to the best of my abilities.

I remained patient because I knew that a lot of different opportunities awaited me as I moved up the school ladder with my grades. My Sanskrit teacher, Mr. Pritam Dev Pamnani, had fallen seriously ill one day. To this day, I am not sure why he would catch an illness every year after the summer break. As it so happened, based on my display of exceptional handling of the Sanskrit language, the school asked me to temporarily step-in and take his place. This decision took me by surprise as I was always told that I was not cut out for this. Nevertheless, I took this newly assigned task head-on.

I may be shy when it came to socializing with others, but I was never shy to work hard. It was the only thing I greeted confidently because I knew I could rely on my capabilities. Becoming a teacher at the age of nineteen only further pushed me into the adult world. Throughout the next six to ten weeks, I began teaching Sanskrit to 8th to 10th graders. Initially, I faced some issues with my *"students"* as they were just a couple of years younger than I was. It was hard for them to take me seriously because they did not see me as an authoritative figure. I was just another kid trying to play the role of an adult to them.

Additionally, it was an overwhelming and challenging opportunity since I was relatively shy and had no public speaking experience whatsoever. There were a lot of fears hiding inside of me. I thought I would fail as a teacher, and it scared me. I went ahead and was not expecting anything extraordinary to happen. However, my predictions were far off. To my surprise, the students loved me after my teaching debut. I enjoyed the temporary role as well because of my love for the subject. I had broken the myth, faced my fears, and triumphed as a result.

The response that I got a few weeks into my teaching career was one that every other teacher aims to have after teaching for decades. My students loved me because I did whatever I could to avoid becoming anything like my 'Punjabi Sir.' I treated my students fairly and taught them well in class that they did not have to take additional tuitions for Sanskrit.

Before fate handed me this opportunity, my teachers didn't encourage me to pursue this aspect due to my reserved nature. Also, after teaching Sanskrit for a couple of months, the same teachers who loved me most as a student had a sudden change in their attitude toward me. I quickly hypothesized that they were probably jealous of me sitting with those who taught me during the breaks. This was my unfortunate first exposure to the wicked world of adults. I realized that teaching might look like a respectable profession, but it wasn't the same case in every other place. It made me realize that just because my teachers were adults did not mean that they were any better than the students they berated from time to time.

They were not spared from the feelings of jealousy like I naively believed. Something might be wrong in the system if a teacher openly becomes jealous of their student's success. After all, we believe that it is the teacher's job to make sure the students excel in all fields in their life. Teachers were supposed to be the catalysts that would speed up their student's success rate, but I was proven wrong based on the experiences I went through.

My children, on the other hand, lived out a childhood that was drastically different from mine. They went through struggles of their own after I moved to Australia. My daughter was only 12-years-old when she was admitted to year seven. She was a brilliant student (just like her father, if I do say so myself). There was a vast difference between the educational systems of Australia and India. Despite her being new to the Australian education system, she performed very well. Within less than a year, she jumped one year ahead and was promoted to year nine at the age of under 13. I am sure she went excessive deep racism at the school but seldom mentioned her experiences with her mother or me. Instead, she chose to ignore the issues and disregarded them as minor problems. She remained focused on her studies and truly believed that her future mattered more than what a few kids had to say about her at her school. At the age of 15, she finished year twelve (the Higher Secondary State Board examination) with highest marks in the entire school and got listed as Dux of 1996.

I believed that my children were not going through major problems since my daughter hardly mentioned her experiences with her. Whenever I would ask her how her day went, she would talk about the good things taking place. However, my son on the other had a different story of his own to share. He was only 7-years-old when we moved to Australia. He struggled with adjusting to the school life in Australia, but quickly got used to the sudden change in environment and developed an interest in sports more than in studies. He picked basketball as his most preferred sport. He was more interested in the NBA than his education.

He had even memorized the complete information on the top NBA players, like Shaq, Michael Jordan, Charles Barkley, Karim Abdul Jabbar, Bill Russell and so on. Moreover, he was collecting cards on several NBA players. In those days, I came across a visiting American family and grew quite close to them. I invited them to my house to introduce my son. I knew they would love him, and my prediction came true.

They were greatly impressed with my son's knowledge of the NBA and decided to let him study in the USA as per my request. They only had one condition that shocked me. They wanted him to convert to Mormonism (Later Day Saints Christianity) otherwise, they wouldn't accept my request. I was flabbergasted by their unreasonable request and refused almost immediately. Religion was one place I wouldn't compromise, no matter what. Though my son was disappointed, he held on to his dreams.

This experience helped me understand how selfish adults can be regarding some matters. I believed that I knew everything I needed to know about the adult world, but I was only proven wrong in the end. That American family had nothing to gain out of my son's conversion to Mormonism except for the fact that they wanted to prove something –whatever that was and to whomever it was directed at. It was as if they believed that anyone would follow along with their whimsical demands as if they were going to grant you a favor. This further proved my theory that adults liked doing favors so that they could hold it over your head for the rest of your life. I did not want anything like that looming over my mind, so I rejected it. Perhaps they thought I would adhere to their unreasonable demands, but I certainly could not.

After three years, I purchased our first house – a large seven rooms house on a thousand yards block of land. By this time, my son was ready for joining the Secondary school. I got him admitted to a private Catholic school called Oakhill College since it was closer to my house. My daughter did not want to change her School and preferred to travel seven kilometers each day.

She was in Higher Secondary School, and she didn't want to go through the hassle of being the new kid in her class One of my biggest mistakes was believing that the schools were going to be impartial to students of all religions. I thought, perhaps naively, that the school system of Australia would focus more on education rather than discrimination. I believed that the teachers here would be different from those back in the home. This blind trust only led my children into one form of despair to another. My son suffered quite prominent cases of open racism at the hands of the teachers, both of whom were Catholic They would disdain other religions as 'minor religions.' This racism adversely affected him greatly, as it would to anyone. It only got worse when his teachers did it so openly in front of other students. It didn't matter whether we were in India or Australia as the flaw lied in the teachers who didn't know what kind of power their words held.

When a teacher tells a student that they will 'never make it' out there in the real world, they don't know how deeply they are affecting their students negatively. A teacher is one of the authoritative figure children look up to, and it only made me realize the power they had over their students.

Most teachers negatively used this power, much to my disdain. Schools are seen as a sacred institution whose primary objective is to educate, nurture, and ultimately produce a polished future generation. It was sad to see it get corrupted so easily.

If I were to start a school, I would make sure that these elements of corruption were kept far from it. The teachers would be well compensated so that they would not feel the need of earning more by giving tuitions on the weekend. I would help other teachers by promoting an environment of teamwork and encouragement. If our children's minds are free of corruption and prejudice, we can be confident that they will grow up to be individuals who reflect honesty and integrity. I learned new things along the way, even after stepping into the adult world.

I learned more about the selfish nature of the people around me as I grew up. I believe that people don't stop growing up after the age of twenty-five or even forty. We all keep learning about new things along the way until we die. I realized that the adult world was a whole lot more complicated than I thought it was going to be. I thought I knew everything I needed to know after I started my own family. Through my children's experiences, I realized that I was far off the mark about understanding the adult world. It made me realize how everyone is seeking to gain something out of other people. Everyone is sticking to their own set of agendas, one way or another.

Emotions like honesty in work were easily disregarded during my time, and they were also overlooked during my children's time. I believe it will continue to be disregarded until everyone notices the importance of bringing a change in the school system. The generation gap did nothing to change the horrific school systems.

Each country had the same values, one way or another, despite having different education boards. I encountered one flaw after another and soon realized that the adult world was too complicated for a simple man like me.

Chapter 2
Hustle to My Success

Adults, unlike children, do not believe in magic. They feel that fairy tales are for youngsters. For them, magic is an escape from the harsh realities of life. This is where children win because deep down, they understand the ideology that magic can be created even in the direst of situations. Perhaps, this is the reason why children always seem happier and more satisfied with life than adults.

I learned early that if I let the morbidity of the adult concepts pull me down, there would remain no difference between an average man and me. Since I had decided, through constant reinforcements from my mother, that I was no ordinary guy, I refused to bow to the practicalities of adulthood. This, I believe, is what kept me going and allowed me to be where I am today.

My venture into the adult world began at the mere age of 16, and it left me contemplating a lot of universal truths. The major one was never to give up, no matter what the world around me continued to think. Following the entire debacle regarding my first adult world exposure, I graduated from high school with flying colors. My mother kept repeating time and time again that I must never let the insecurities of the adults around me hinder my path. It is one of those pieces of advice I still stick to and have imparted to my own children as well. I have learned in time that people continue to stir hate and negativity, no matter how further apart you try to keep yourself. Therefore, the only way to remain unaffected is to continue moving on and doing the best you can.

I won't lie and claim that this attitude of bleakness did not pull me down, but I refused to let it keep me that way. I knew I wanted to achieve something from my life, something big, and I refused to let smaller people stop me from getting to my target. I knew I had the will as well as the brain to make it big.

It was in school when I realized that Sanskrit was not the only subject I excelled at. All the hard work that my mother and I had put in my home education had paid off, and I had discerned that I was really good at studies, particularly in the subjects such as mathematics, physics, and analytical chemistry. In those times, if you were good at these subjects, it meant a world of excellent academic means were open for you in India.

Hence, after graduating from high school, I joined a college to pursue my degree in engineering. Within a few days, my peers and teachers alike discovered my hidden talent in the subject mentioned above. Solving problems in mathematics and physics was something I quickly gained recognition for in college. Not only my friends, but other fellow students would also line up to get my help with solving complex mathematical problems.

This was an immense boost to my ego. It also gave me the confidence to pursue my education with vigor and hard work. I always knew that I could achieve whatever I set my mind to, but college made me revel in the thought that I truly was good at what mattered. Let's be clear. I was not a prodigy who would look at any algebraic equation or trigonometric problem at hand and answer within minutes.

Instead, most times, I would get caught in the difficulty of the problem and would need a good night's sleep to come up with an accurate answer. My friends and fellowmen used to laugh at this distinct gift where I would sleep on a problem and come up with a solution the next day. This seemed a rather strange yet pleasing thing to me. However, I never gave it too much thought – simply choosing to enjoy the banter of my class fellows.

In my school, my old competitors and friends returned to college, too. Meera was back, as was the rivalry and competition of who got the topmost marks. Even though she stayed only two years in the same university as me before moving out to the City of Bombay, these two years taught me a lot about competition, corruption within education, and how racist teachers could destroy the lives of students with a single word from their mouth.

It seemed that Meera was created by God to become an obstacle to my education, but I say this in a good way. Had she not been around to challenge my superiority, I would never have learned that everything does not come from hard work only. Rather, a few things need to be achieved with smart work.

Even though I loved all other sciences, I never truly understood or liked biology. Of course, that meant Meera absolutely loved it and excelled at it, too. This also meant that this was the only subject she would get more marks in than me. I worked extremely hard to beat her and attain top marks. However, even though I got a good score in the quarterly (exams that took place every three months), it seemed that no matter what I did, she would come out the winner in the end.

One day, around six months since the start of term, I gathered up the courage to go and request that Meera show me her work. She did not hesitate even for a minute and showed me her papers with a proud flourish. What I noticed took me aback. Her answers or explanations were not really that different than the ones I had written. The only exception was that she had filled her journal with large pictures and well spread out text. In other words, there was only the difference in presentation. Hers was obviously better than mine. I vowed to do the same from then on, and to my pleasant surprise, things turned for the better immediately.

My marks jumped up substantially. Interestingly enough, Meera did not perform all that well in the annual exams of the university, which meant that both she and I scored almost the same. Since I was already better at mathematics and physics, my overall grade in the exam was higher than hers, so that I achieved around 10% better grades than her. But this, sadly, was not where my woes ended. It was not only biology that Meera did better compared to me. She also always got better marks in organic chemistry. This upset me a lot because from what I could see, as we were equally good at the subject.

Yet, it was always her who scored the winning number. It was here when I came face to face with corruption among authority yet again. In school, I had already faced discrimination due to my gender, as well as caste. The same was the case in college. Even though the first year passed relatively quietly, the second year of college was the one that I like to think of as one of the toughest of my life. Not only did I discover that my family's finances were deteriorating rapidly, but I also became aware of teachers' corruption.

We were taught biology and chemistry by a very tall and handsome man, who sadly got into a relationship with my beautiful adversary. Meera had another friend who shared her name, and the two girls were always hounding our handsome biology lecturer. I do not know if they truly cared about him, but his involvement was wrong, and he knew it. Since there was no one to contest this, things kept on going unchecked.

Meera and her friend would frequently visit the lecturer's room on the pretext that they needed help with the subjects. Of course, the lecturer, being a man with raging hormones, insured that both the girls obtained brilliant grades on his subjects. This meant that Meera always scored higher than me – not only in biology but also organic chemistry.

As frustrating as it was for me, there was literally nothing I could do about this. I was left with no choice but to wonder about how the corruption of our education system was robbing rightful students from gaining the accomplishments they deserved. It was a sad reality that was deeply seated in our customs, and there seemed no end to it. I, at least, had the conviction that I was better than Meera because she was gaining good marks due to her special favors while I did everything on my own. In our second year of college, a new principal was appointed, Dr. Bhagwat, who belonged to the Marathi ethnicity.

Marathis are the local community that belongs to the State of Maharashtra. They are one of the oldest communities in India, as well as one of the most influential. Their number is huge, and their language and literature are one of the oldest and the most diverse. Perhaps, this is one of the reasons why Marathi people feel a sense of entitlement and pride in their customs and language. Dr. Bhagwat was a well-educated man. This meant he had a good influence over matters of the university. However, this, I felt, is where his commendations ended. Dr. Bhagwat was one of the narrowest minded and racist people I had ever met in my life.

He felt that only Marathis should have access to the best of the best in terms of education and everything else that the State of Maharashtra had to offer. Everyone else, no matter what ethnicity they belonged to, were like second-grade citizens in his eyes. He did not feel they had the right to success and should not have access to any high position in the state. It needs to be stated again that the college was owned and mostly run by Sindhis, yet he sparked a divide among the students.

As I mentioned earlier, Dr. Bhagwat was highly educated and an accomplished teacher of inorganic chemistry. No matter what people think about him, everyone accepted that he was brilliant at what he did. Students loved the way he was able to simplify even the most complex topics of inorganic chemistry. No matter how much of a dunce the student was, they would be able to understand whatever Dr. Bhagwat explained.

The only problem was, Dr. Bhagwat was dead set against Sindhis. He felt they were refugees from Pakistan who had no place in India. He missed no opportunity to mock the Sindhi students. He would try to insult and demean them every time he could, which was pretty much every day. When talking about ethane or methane, he would say things like, *"Remember it is 'e' at the end, not 'I'; otherwise it will become an Ethani, a Sindhi..."* But this was where the humor of the situation ended. It was because of his racism and derogatory comments that Marathis would stay away from everyone, particularly Sindhis. This created a rift among students and staff alike. Since Sindhis had no such qualms, they would remain friendly toward everyone, but Marathi students changed during the reign of Dr. Bhagwat. As I learned in the upcoming days, things only got from bad to worse.

According to our academic requirements, in order to get into good engineering and medical colleges, we needed high scores in the annual examinations of our second-year session. This is where Dr. Bhagwat became a problem and probably destroyed the career of many budding scholars. He moved very carefully and, by using his contacts with the high officials of the education department, ensured that no Sindhi students did well. He provided the board with a list of prominent Sindhi students who were to be punished for being who they were, as well as another list of Marathi students who were to be favored for the same reason. This was a huge blow for all the good Sindhi students in the second year.

Since I usually hung around with my Sindhi friends, I too was included in the list of Sindhi students. The only good thing that came out of this for me, I feel, was that it did not matter to me whether I was favored or not. I had already found out that I would not be able to continue my studies in engineering due to family concerns and financial strains. However, this still impacted my thought process and the illusion I had about education and educationists.

This is the problem with everything we are working toward. Teachers continue to forget that their status and approach is wide and detrimental, which is why they need to be excessively careful with how they use it. If they continue to abuse the power they hold, many amazing scholars will be lost at a point where they need support the most. If it was not for the handsome biology lecturer and Dr. Bhagwat, other deserving students would have been able to excel and become accomplished people in their lives. However, the injustice of academia is unparalleled.

As entertaining and enlightening as college life was, it was not without its own set of hardships. It was not long before I was thrown back into the problems of the past where my father was becoming incapable of feeding nine members of the family. He had been salvaging for the past innumerable years in trying to make sure that our family was fed, clothed, and secure, but now he was becoming weak with age and exhaustion. It was difficult for me to watch as a bystander while he continued to suffer. I knew that my family's financial condition was getting to the point where I needed to step in and take charge. I could see from the direction of the winds that my elder brother had no prospects and no goals to follow, not truly bothered by what was happening to our loved ones. This meant that it would fall on me, as the second eldest son of the family to become the breadwinner.

I did what I knew best at that point. I became a part-time teacher at one of the high schools, while also offering tuitions to a few students who were in school and college. This was an eye-opener for me because it was at this point that I began to understand what the worth of education and good teachers was. I had learned early that good teachers, who were fair and just to all their students, were only a few and far between. I understood the importance of any teacher's guidance and care given to students as I had suffered at the hands of the corrupt who only seemed to care about their selfish motives, not the benefit of the young students.

Hence, I made sure that I put my heart and soul in teaching in the best manner I could. The resultant results were apparent immediately. My students flourished under my strict eyes. I still remember their shining eyes when they accomplished success in their respective academic career. Even though I had to work part-time while I was in college, those two years were some of the best ones I had.

It was these two years that taught me about my strengths. I accepted the fact that hard work was unavoidable, and if I did it with heart, I would be rewarded tenfold. I was humbled by the gifts that nature had granted me and vowed to help anyone I could to the best of my skills. Once I successfully completed my two years at the science college, I knew that there wasn't much choice but to run after a full-time career.

It was my deepest desire to study engineering, but that

was not an option for me because engineering universities required full daytime attendance, which was something I could not give. As I explained before, the finances of my family were dwindling fast, and my father was growing weary of all the responsibilities. This meant that somebody needed to become the major burden bearer. Who else was left but me? It was with a heavy heart that I decided to let go of my aspirations for engineering.

There simply was no other choice. This is what led to the decision of changing my majors from Science to Advanced Economics. I decided to apply for English Literature and Applied Statistics, too, in addition to the major I was already taking. It seemed that these subjects would come in handy for whatever career I turned to in the unforeseen future.

Now that I look back on my chosen academic path, I feel the main reason for choosing English Literature was that my father was well versed in English and placed great emphasis on its importance. Our colonial mindset comes to the surface as Indians had always been inspired by English and to them, becoming fluent in English language and its custom would open doors like nothing else.

I can say with an honest conscience that in my case, English Literature did help with shaping my personality and thoughts to be like how they are today. My mind has broadened letting me think outside the box because of the decisions I took about my education.

Therefore, as soon as the first two years of college concluded, I decided to secure a job, all the while looking for other ways to get closer to engineering. I admit that the thought of studying science never left my mind. I loved the subjects too much and understood them too well for me not to give them up completely at that point. This is the reason that I was always on the lookout for opportunities that would put me somewhere near the field of engineering. When such a choice arrived, I jumped at it. After the extreme struggle, I was able to appear in the entrance examination of a large engineering corporation by the name of Larsen & Toubro Limited in Bombay. This entrance exam would allow me to get my hands on a four-year apprenticeship position with this prestigious company. I remember the excitement and happiness I felt on this feat. It was like I was given another prospect to go after my dream of becoming an engineer.

The position I secured was a full eight-hour job, where

four hours were restricted to theory in a classroom, while the remaining four hours were to be spent in the factory workshop, learning the practical art of engineering. It was a session that I couldn't wait to begin. On the very first day of the job, we were required to take six progressive tests that were based on multiple choice questions. Each test seemed to become harder and harder than the one before it. At every level of the tests, a few of the candidates were eliminated from the engineering program due to their poor performance.

It took the entire day for these tests to end – somewhere around six hours. At the start of the session, there were about 30 candidates, and by the time the day came to an end, we had shrunk to merely five people. I, luckily, was among those five candidates. It was explained that we would be required to appear the next day for the practical part of the entrance test. I remained in high spirits, knowing that if I could get through the theory, I would also be able to pass the practical.

It seemed as though my bad luck was not going to leave me and that engineering would continue to elude me. The day of the theory exam, I got a chance to eat at the huge corporate canteen that boasted the ambiance of a five-star restaurant and served food of the most excellent quality. The food, which was very hygienic and tasted superb, was basically South Indian, as the majority of workers at the firm, some 3000 plus, were all South Indian.

I had never before eaten any kind of South Indian meal and was, therefore, tasting it for the very first time. I found it delicious and probably consumed more than I should have. The result became apparent on my return home. I became severely sick with diarrhea. It got so bad that all my energy was sapped out of me, and I became extremely dehydrated. By the next morning, I had become so weak that I was unable to get off the bed without the help of my mother. There was no other choice. I just couldn't go to work in this condition, nor could I give any kind of practical exam. This meant that I needed to inform the authority of my ailment. I called up Laron & Toubro, requesting that they rescheduled my practical test. Surprisingly enough, the company representative refused point-blank, stating that it was not their policy to reschedule tests. What was even worse though was that they told me I would not be allowed to reapply for the position ever again. I could not have been more devastated at this news.

Had it not been the support and encouragement of my mother, I would most definitely have fallen in depression and hopelessness. By that time, I had not given up completely, but I had been dealt a severe blow about the harsh realities of life. My mother persuaded me to look elsewhere for similar positions. So I did and found out that other large engineering companies, such as Tata Engineering, also offered similar tests and positions. Sadly, I was rejected everywhere because of my weak physique. They said I would not be able to keep up with the laborious work of the engineering sector.

I cannot express how great a blow this was for me. I had never truly lost at anything that I had worked hard for, but this time, I was shown by fate that not everything can be achieved with dedication and hard work. Some things come through luck and chance, too.

It was at this point that I came to the conclusion that engineering was just not meant for me. Hence, I let go of my passion for engineering and dedicated my time and efforts to what I could accomplish with the subjects at hand, meaning Economics, Allied Statistics, and English Literature. Hence, I ended up majoring in Economics with Allied Statistics and English Literature as minors for my graduation.

This combination of education and work meant that I would get up early in the morning for my college classes and go to work in the afternoon once college ended. By the time I came home, it would be a 12-hour shift. I would then complete my homework and study for exams. The 12 plus working/study hours became a norm for me that I soon became used to. One reason might be that I was not new to this grueling, hard work.

I settled down, accepted my fate, and decided to make sure that I excelled at what I was doing at the time. It took some time to adjust, but I did learn to accept what I had at hand. This acceptance calmed me, allowing me to succeed and prosper. And this is exactly what has led me to where I am today.

Chapter 3
Corruption Prevails

People say that life changes when you grow up. I didn't truly believe it until I reached adulthood with my job at a bank. It was then that I realized what it meant to really grow and learned that life, as we know, is only a misconception. It was the 2nd June of 1969 when I joined the Central Bank of India in Bombay. At that time, this bank was believed to be one of the top three largest private sector banks in India, which made people admire it a lot As a result, many of my acquaintances were not impressed with me, but rather jealous of my position.

Te Central Bank was one of those thirteen top private sector banks that were nationalized by then Prime Minister, Indira Gandhi, on 20th July 1969. Nationalization of an institution means that it is forcibly acquired by the government, regardless of whether the institution wishes to be a state-owned enterprise or not. I clearly remember that most people who were a part of the bank were not happy with this shift. A few months later, I vividly remember one line from the speech of the Chairman of the Bank, *"Yesterday, the man reached the moon and today, a woman has done something to the Indian banking."*

People were aggravated by this move and blamed the woman PM of India for this transition in the system, which they felt would lower the banking experience. This was the time when I learned that promotion prospects at the Central Bank of India were not at all good and that the Bank of India would be a much better employment option if it was progress you were after. This caused me to begin reconsidering my choice. Was I willing to waste my time at a place where I would remain at the same junior position for a long time? No chance of promotion or consideration? Probably with no new learning either? Or do I want something different? I decided against this fallacy and, within three months, switched my job.

On the 6th of October 1969, I became a part of the Bank of India located across the Mahatma Gandhi Road. Even though I had joined at a beginner's position as a clerk, the prospects of getting a quick promotion were bright. I did not know this at that moment, but this was the place that would help me leave my positive delusions behind and become the thinking and introspecting man I am today. The bank, its employees, and my experiences working there have taught me life lessons that have allowed me to deal with multiple complicated situations and come out unharmed. The best part is that I made some really good friends at the bank. Here is a detailed account of what my life was like in the Bank of India. As I have explained before, I had started working from a very early age. By the time I got to my banking position, I was only a naïve 20-year-old. This meant that even though I had seen the face of corruption and human ugliness, I still did not know the extent to which it had penetrated our collective mindset. And this was something that I was face to face with in this new position.

I was still under the impression that people meant what they said and said what they meant. The duplicity and sarcasm were unimaginable for me, and it took a lot of time for me to understand the wickedness of the human soul. Evil, by its nature, is bound to surface, and I was able to experience first-hand the corruption of the officials in senior positions. The eye-opening realization was not pleasant, but it made me aware of my surroundings. To this day, I refuse to accept the derogatory norm, '*it's human nature,*' '*everyone wants to be one up,*' '*everyone is selfish,*' etc. I believe the people who accept these explanations are the reason why corruption prevails.

It is because of them that progress becomes stagnant, and there is no cleansing in society. Even though I was working full-time for the bank, I was also studying at a university part-time. However, I felt this was not enough and in order to advance in my banking career, I would need other, more technical qualifications and certifications. Hence, the reason why I started other professional studies for a banking diploma with the Indian Institute of Bankers, and later with the British Institute of Bankers for an advanced diploma.

While all these diplomas were ongoing, I was also completing my Bachelor of Arts with a major in Economics and Applied Statistics. Once that was done, I began a degree in Commerce (Advanced Accounting and Auditing) that lasted for two more years and got me a university degree – a Bachelor of Commerce with Honors.

As if this was not enough, I also started pursuing professional studies in Cost and Management Accountancy from the Institute of Cost and Management Accountants of India. I completed my degree with distinction. While all of my academic achievements were going on, my career had not stopped. When I was in the bank, I got to work in a variety of departments – from the head office to the main branch. This meant that I was shuffled from one place to the other a lot. As much as it aggravated me in those times, now that I look back, I feel that this was what opened my eyes to the reality of people. Everywhere I went, there were nepotism and favoritism. The shock was pretty real at first, so much so that I was unable to reel back. However, eventually, I learned to ignore it, or at least not to affect me too much. I just could not understand why people were the way they were and why they didn't see the dishonesty behind their actions. It was like all sense of fairness and justice was lost, and even the nicest person seemed to be hiding a face behind their façade.

Eventually, I became too busy with my work and studies to care much or take notice. The one thing I did was keep out of other people's way and focus on my job. This helped with taking my mind off the corruption of the senior officials. I was put in the general reserve of staff portfolio and did not have a permanent department. I was mostly shifted to a different one every week, even though there were times when I had to shuffle from one department to the next every single day. Even though this was slightly uncomfortable, I gained invaluable experience working under different bosses in a variety of departments. I was finally put in a department that was headed by a woman. This was an oddity in itself. It may not seem like a big deal to you now, but you have to look at things from the perspective of that time. It was early 70's in India, which meant that women were meant to stay home, look after the kids, and not work in offices alongside men, let alone work as their superiors. This meant that women who were in positions of power were looked down upon and made fun of. They had to exert a lot of pressure and authority for them to even be taken seriously.

It was a similar situation in our department as most men would laugh behind her back, making fun of the way she ran things. She had to keep a strict demeanor in order to subdue such men. But I respected her and did not talk behind her back. I appreciated the fact that her hard work had gotten her where she was, which is why I adhered to all her rules.

She, of course, found this very odd, as no one else reacted in a similar manner in the department. She had expected the same kind of behavior from me as my colleagues. When she saw no such thing coming forward, she would look strangely at me, but did not make a remark. She would continue to be suspicious of me and would eye me peculiarly – as if trying to understand me. After some time, though, she realized that I was different and genuinely respected her. This led her to forgo her present reserve and hesitation. She started appreciating my stance and became very nice. However, I feel she continued to think that I was a weird guy. It was Mr. Chemburkar, an officer in the bank, whose kindness and consideration made a lasting impression on my mind. I will never forget all that he did for me during my tenure at the bank and how, if it was not for him, I would have never gained the confidence I did. Mr. Chemburkar was my senior and worked in the same department. He was a father to five daughters, whom he loved very much, and still felt the absence of a son, which is why he treated me like his own flesh and blood.

He could see that I was working to the bone and would not only sympathize, but also appreciate my efforts. He saw that my education, along with the full-time job, was draining me of energy. Hence, he made sure that I took time off work, during working hours to have some time to recuperate from the stress of it all. He would force me to take a few hours off and spend it outside of the office. I would go to the cinema and watch movies at matinee shows, making sure I was always back by lunchtime.

I can say this without a doubt that had it not been for Mr. Chemburker, I would have collapsed under the pressure of trying to maintain a job and continue my education. The work was not merely hard, it was mind-numbly exhausting. I was left with no time to release the stress because I was either at the bank working or at the university attempting to gain my educational degrees. The few hours that my kind mentor forced me to take off were what kept me going. They helped me forget the hardships I was facing and allowed me a respite when I needed it the most. I will forever be grateful to that considerate gentleman who appeared in my life at a point when I needed him the most.

A new phase of my life started as I completed thirty months of my employment with the Bank of India. The bank finally took notice of my efforts and decided to send me for a special training program that would last a full eight weeks. I was not sent to any other city but was required to visit the training center on the other side of the town in a picturesque locality that was close to the sea. This meant that I was required to travel about 45 minutes by bus from the main train station of Victoria Terminus. I did not mind the long commute as it meant that the bank was finally letting me learn their trade.

The journey was extraneous, but it would improve my chances of success and career advancement. It was at this point in time when I met a co-worker, Durga. She was nicknamed Papu, and all those people who were close to her would refer to her by that name. She belonged to an old and rich Sindhi family who were goldsmith by profession. I had previously known Durga in university when we were classmates in the second year, but we never had a chance to interact. During my two years of university, we had not exchanged a word with one another.

Since the training required both of us to travel every day together for the next eight weeks, we ended up communicating. This conversation led to a good friendship and later, we fell deeply in love with each other. We shared similar ideas and beliefs, and this is what brought us closer to each other.

Durga was a tall, beautiful, and extremely good-natured girl, who would go out of her way to be friendly and kind to everyone. This was perhaps the reason why she was such a favorite among everyone in her department. She worked in the Personal or Human Resources department, and her friendliness caused everyone to love her there.

Compared to Durga, I was not at all a looker in those days. I was of slight stature, and there did not seem to be anything striking about me. She told me that her department colleagues did not like me and kept telling her that I was not a suitable match for her. This caused a lot of consternation for me, and even though I was disheartened, there was not much I could do about the situation. I knew I could not stop loving her, but I also could not make people like me as I did not have the time or the energy to do anything about my looks. However, the spark of positivity here was that nothing seemed to make her lose interest in me. She told me time and time again that it did not matter to her what people thought about me as her love was too strong.

And I believed her completely. As I have said previously, the people in her department thought we were not suitable for each other. They worked hard to make sure that I was put in the general reserve. Durga did not like this and requested her manager to remove me from this position as soon as possible. She ensured that her manager put me in a decent department permanently so I would not regularly shuffled around. The manager obliged her, and because of this, I was posted in the department of Fixed Deposits, which was the one where the lady boss who I previously mentioned was present. Issues started when there was talk of Durga and me getting married. It was three years after I had met and fallen in love with her when Durga's mother got her engaged to a Sindhi guy from her caste of goldsmiths. Suffice it to say that I was heartbroken and Durga was forced into the situation through emotional blackmail.

I went to meet her widowed mother, grandfather, and uncles to ask for her hand in marriage, but they refused to listen to even a word I said. I told them time and time again about my love for Durga and how I would keep her happy. They kept saying no because according to them, they did not allow marriages out of caste. This meant that no matter how Durga or I felt, she would have to marry the Sindhi boy.

This was another time in my life when I realized that it was money that made the world go round. If you were wealthy, you could take over everything and everyone. If you were not, you were left to struggle throughout life. What's more, the worth of a person was judged based on the family they came from, along with how much money was in their name. I cannot explain how this blow shook me. Not only was I losing the love of my life, but I was also being degraded for not being Sindhi and for not being rich.

All my efforts to make something of myself were disregarded, and I was left as someone who did not deserve positivity in life. Durga's younger sister was a student of mine when I was teaching at the school on a part-time basis. I was also friends with her younger brother, who liked me a lot. Both of these younger siblings wanted to see me with Durga, knowing we were in love and wanted us to get married. Unfortunately, nothing they said in my defense made any difference.

While these struggles were taking place, Durga told me that her younger sister had run away with a classmate of hers, who was also from a different caste. She knew her family would never allow their union, so she chose to flee. It had upset her family a lot and made Durga miserable. She resolved in front of me that she will never do that to her family and widowed mother. She knew that they would not be able to handle her betrayal.

This is how our three-year relationship ended. Since we both knew nothing would happen, we stopped seeing each other altogether. I heard and saw with my own eyes how happy Durga's manager and colleagues were at our breakup. They never wanted to see us together, and their dream had come true without any endeavor on their part. I felt further humiliated. Was I really so terrible for the gorgeous Durga that even her colleagues were happy at us losing touch? Did my capabilities make me nothing? I have to admit that the loss of someone I loved broke me in a million ways. I could not believe the harshness of life. It was not the first time a girl's family had rejected me, but it was the first time I had begun to doubt myself. It was like I simply was not good enough.

My mother had always told me that if you worked hard and established yourself, success inevitably came your way. However, this rule did not seem to apply to me. I was losing all the things that were most important for me, and there was nothing I was able to do about it. The gloom did not last long. I was not the kind of person who gave up too easily. I pushed myself even more deeply into work.

I accepted the fact that people would continue to use and abuse me whenever and wherever I let them. The only means of persevering is by concentrating on what matters the most. In my case, it was my education and work. I would work hard and make something of myself, no matter who thought what. Never again would I give anyone the chance to hurt or rattle me. This is what helped me succeed in building a stellar career for myself. From there on, I did not allow anyone to shake my faith in myself. I knew of my strengths and weaknesses, and only I would be the master of them. This new resolution filled me up with newfound hope and determination.

The lesson I learned in this phase of my life was not to pay any heed to the prejudices of people, but to keep yourself in mind. No one in the entire world knows you better than you. So let no one deter you from your path to excellence. Believe that in time you will reach your path.

Chapter 4
The Bank of India

Within three years at the Bank of India, I was promoted to an officer's position. Around that time, the bank had implemented a new system under which it created several regions and regional offices. One such office was the Bombay Metropolitan Office, which had 101 banking branches. I was posted at that office and was made in charge of the newly created Statistical Cell within it.

My job was to collect weekly information from the 101 branches they had on their key performance indicators in bank deposits, loans, advances, and *"Sick and Nursing industrial units."* I would then collate the information collected from different branches and present a consolidated regional report to the Regional Manager. This was a place I learned a lot from, but it was not the only thing that I got in touch with. I also realized that I was in a position where I was exposed to a lot of power, one that is automatically gained when you are in association with someone who is in power. Since I needed to report to the authority about my data collection, I was very close to the Regional Manager of the bank.

This closeness also meant that many people did not like my position of authority and doubted the credibility that was assigned to me. There were just too many branch managers that I had to question – in terms of official stance on data of course, but question all the same. These were people who had been working for the bank longer, had more experience, and even earned a lot more than I did. Some earned ten to fifteen times more than what I made at that time. Yet, all these senior employees had to answer to me, and this caused a lot of embarrassment for me.

I know for a fact that these senior managers became awkward and resentful at my inquiries, even though none of them let it be apparent. Whenever I would call a branch manager, reminding them that I needed information, the manager would become very apologetic and promise to send the information as soon as possible. They would also request that I not relay the information to the Regional Manager because they had obviously not done the work on time that was expected of them. This was an extremely tricky place for me to be in. Imagine being the junior most employee, and dealing with other employees who were not just senior, but also had been in the business for a longer time. Seeing their discomfort made me similarly uncomfortable, and all I wanted to do was fade away from the picture. But there wasn't much I could do about the situation, challenging as it was. Therefore, I continued on with the arduous task of getting data out of corrupt officers. The one person who supported and encouraged me and who stands out in my memory was the Regional Manager of the time, Mr. Rego. He was the one who reminded me that I was no less an employee, and if I was given a job, it must mean that the superiors thought I was capable of handling it well.

Therefore, there was no need for me to either feel bad or embarrassed. Mr. Rego was a Christian from Goa, and he was the one person in the office, who seemed to like me a lot and was genuinely kind to me. Moreover, he didn't simply just like me as person, but approved of how efficient I was. Since he understood my embarrassment, he told me to remain, frank, brave, and firm with the way I talked to senior officers. As I have already mentioned, the managers resented my inqusitive position, and hence, there were many times that many of them would not comply with my request for data collection.

It got to the point, at times, where I was left hanging helplessly, not knowing what should be done as people would consider me too insignificant to respond. It was Mr. Rego who stressed that I should report these people who would not transfer the information I needed. Since I too had people who worked in various branches, I was told that the branch manager would ensure my calls were stood up, not answered or delayed, whenever I would officially make the call, asking for information.

This assured me that there was no point in saving them or keeping their names hidden because all that was happening was that I was the one getting delayed for transfer of information. Hence, instead of the people responsible, I was the one getting blamed for something that wasn't my fault, to begin with. This was the time that I decided enough was enough and that I wouldn't try to 'save' people.

If there is one thing I learned from this experience, it was that intimidation of authority only leads to failure. The less you were afraid of them, the less likely they were to threaten you. And surprisingly enough, this worked well in my case. At the time, I was dealing with this personal drama, the government has introduced several priority sectors to lend money to various businesses, such as small industries, small agricultural units, small businesses, etc.

The nationalized banks were required to lend up to 25% of their total lending portfolio. Each branch was required to report on priority sector lending. This is the early times we are talking about, which mean that there were no emails or computer systems. Since there was no standard reporting format for the branches to report, it meant that people would find it easy to miss reports, delay them, or even conveniently forget to type them up. All information needed to be prepared manually, and faxed as soon as it was relayed. Unfortunately, in most situations, this wasn't done at all.

I soon realized the predicament of the branches and decided to do something to solve this problem. This is what led to my developing and designing a standard reporting format based on my experience with the branches. Interestingly enough, the Regional Manager liked the idea and suggested that it should be introduced nationally to all bank regions. With his approval, I immediately introduced the format for my region, the Bombay Metropolitan Region, and submitted my format to the Organizational & Methods Department at the National Head Office. They approved it and with a few minor modifications, introduced the format nationwide.

I was rewarded with a small cash prize, which ruffled a lot of feathers in the regional offices. This was another feather to my hat. I could now hold my own because not only did I knew my job well, I was capable enough to come up with new ideas and have them implemented into the old system.

Some other people who have left a mark in my memory are deputy regional managers, Mr. Daru and Mr. Manjeshwar. They also liked me a lot and we got along really well. Mr. Daru was a Parsi gentleman who I think liked me because I was so young yet efficient at what I did. He thought that I did more work than the rest of the managers put together. He, too, always encouraged mc to focus on what I was doing, paying no attention to the jealous and incompetent senior officers.

My position came with some perks. I had a staff of 7, which included two stenographer secretaries. Unlike others in the bank, I did not believe in displaying authority and ruling with power or cruelty. My aim was to ensure that the people who worked under me were happy and loyal to me. In my own experience, when you are happy with the management, you can adapt to work better and giving your best. And most importantly, people who had good managers, or were friendly with them – these were the ones who remained loyal till the end and did everything they could to ensure the manager had all the work disposed off in time. Hence, the reason why I kept a friendly and amiable presence. I would never exhibit any of my authority over my staff, and in return, they did their work efficiently and loved me back, too. At this point, there were a total of three boys and four girls who worked for me.

The only person who didn't respond to my affectionate manner was a Christian girl named Mary. She would neither answer back, nor would she ever try to become friendly. I felt that she was a little snobbish and rude, considering I had a gentle attitude even though others in my position would have behaved differently.

One day, I was talking to another Christian girl in the department and expressed my thoughts on how Mary seemed to act so strangely. This girl told me that the reality was quite different. The only reason why Mary was the way she was with me was that she was actually in love with me. I was shocked to hear this, particularly because people who were in love did not really behave in such a weird manner. The girl told me that even though Mary loved me dearly, she was very scared of her elder brother, who had warned her against falling in love with or getting in a relationship with anyone other than a Christian guy. Her brother had strictly warned her that he would never allow her to marry out of the sect and since he worked in the same building, the secret would be out faster than she could utter ‘I love you.’ And this was the reason that Mary kept her distance from me. She could not afford to get close to me and have her brother discover her closely guarded secret. I felt really bad for Mary after this and kept my distance too.

I obviously knew what it felt like to have a broken heart and didn’t want her to experience a similar fate. The poor girl was already miserable, and I did not want to make things even tougher for her. I have already told you previously that I was a very thin lad. This was the reason I had to give up my dream of becoming an engineer. However, even though such a tragedy had taken place in my life, I simply did not have the time or energy to pay attention to my physique.

I still looked really weak, weighing a mere 52 kilograms with my height of 5 feet 10 inches. This, I feel, is one of the reasons that people seemed to underestimate my capabilities because I looked so slight and non-dominating.

But something changed all this. It was the four weeks I took off from work to prepare for my university finals. Since I needed to study all the time, I took a leave from work for a month and spent all my time preparing for the upcoming exams. As I was immersed in studies all the time, my mother took it upon herself to ensure that I ate well. She would not only feed me rich foods but would also give me extra mind and health-boosting tidbits all the time. One thing she started giving me daily were almonds soaked overnight in water, peeled, and then consumed the next day.

In India, it is believed that these almonds help in boosting brain power. I don't know if they boost brain powers, but they, along with rich foods, did help me gain about 20 kilograms in a few weeks. This meant that from a measly 52 kilos, I suddenly was 72 kilos. The fat was in all the right places since I was already particular about my exercise regimen, and it meant I looked extremely appealing.

I found new confidence in the way I looked and decided to contact Durga once again. Even though she was engaged at that time, we started going out once more. But our love affair this time around was really short lived as Durga's mother found out and got her married off immediately. She still refused to accept me, even though I had grown good looking and was doing really well at work, too. I wouldn't say this incident shattered me because I was already used to getting rejected by Durga's family. Just like the affair with Durga, my privilege at the bank was short-lived, too – only two years. After that, the Regional Manager, Mr. Rego, was transferred to a senior post. The new Regional Manager, Mr. Karnik, was a staunch Maharashtrian and a typical bureaucrat who strongly believed in seniority over efficiency. On top of that, he was also a racist who believed that only Maharashtrian speaking Marathi people should be in positions of importance. This meant that he did not like me at all. He would say I was too junior to deal with the branch managers who were senior to me.

Therefore, he ended up bringing one of his own close followers, Dr. Joshi, who had a doctorate degree in Statistics. Dr. Joshi was over thirty years my senior and drawing a salary that was at least 10-12 times that of mine. I was made his assistant, doing the same work However, I was reporting to Dr. Joshi instead of the Regional Manager. Dr. Joshi would not let me meet the Regional Manager alone or even engage with the two Deputy Regional

Managers. One Deputy Regional Manager, Mr. Daru, still preferred to talk to me directly – he would always walk to my seat for any information or call me to his office.

Soon, Mr. Karnik managed to transfer two senior branch managers, both Gujaratis of course, named D Desai and A Desai to the Regional Office. Mr. D Desai was the senior most of the two and hence, was made Assistant Regional Manager, reporting directly to the Regional Manager. I was required to report to him for some of the work I did, in addition to Dr. Joshi. These two branch managers were the ones who would make sure that my calls went unanswered whenever I was required to extract data from them when they were branch managers. I realized quickly enough that they felt embarrassed to see me, discovering that I was far more *"junior"* to them. I also came to know that they were very close to the Regional Manager as far as their roles and duties were concerned. This meant they were basically nothing more than his very own personal obedient servants.

All of this would not have mattered to me, but after some time, they started giving me a really hard time even though they would play as if they were really nice to me. A Desai would act like he was my one true well-wisher and best friend but would backstab me the moment he had the chance. I had to visit Assistant Regional Manager D Desai frequently, and many times A Desai was already there with him, talking about one thing or the other with regards to what I might have done. One day, I was sitting in D Desai's room for some work when A Desai entered the room. He didn't notice me and instantly upon entering the room, started spouting vitrol against me. I still remember that incident when he said in Gujarati, *"Sir Mr. Watts is very bad man and must be punished severely."* D Desai pointed at me to indicate that I was in the room as well, and they both went quiet for some time. A Desai felt embarrassed but didn't say sorry to me. I had no choice but to ignore that incident However, this put me on alert, and I became very cautious while talking to A Desai.

Both realized that Mr. Daru, Deputy Regional Manager, liked me a lot and would not listen to anything against me. This, therefore, made them stop speaking against me in front of him at the very least. At that time, Mr. Daru was the only person who was my actual well-wisher. He was the only one who would encourage and support me, even at times when others decided to keep their distance from me. Other officers, though friendly with me, would not dare say anything in my support in front of the two Desais because they were worried about what wrath would befall them if they spoke anything in my defense.

I did not blame any of them as they had a right to behave that way. After all, everyone was concerned about their job security. This showed me the ugly face of bureaucracy in India. Around the same time when the two Desias were playing tricks with me, trying to discredit me in any way possible, violent communal riots erupted in Bombay's CBD and suburbs. The ethnic Marathi fanatic community group called Shiv Sena started ransacking the main roads, shops, and other establishments.

They wanted to own all businesses as a matter of their birth right, as everything was located in the vicinity they occupied. They would apprehend anyone on the streets or traveling in buses and trains and start speaking in Marathi. If the person did not respond in Marathi, he would be severly beaten. Due to such dangerous conditions, most trains and buses were canceled.

This carnage lasted continuously for more than seven days. I could not travel to Bombay to attend my duties at the office for five days straight. Conseqeuntly, I had to get special permission to work in a small local branch close to my house as that would not require any kind of traveling. This perhaps was the moment that both the Desais were waiting for. They decided to get rid of me from the Bombay office. D Desai approached Mr. Daru, the Deputy Regional Manager, who had always liked me, telling him that I was asking for a transfer to the branch near my house. This was as far from the truth as could have been as I had never asked for such a favor. I was perfectly happy working where I was planted. But Mr. Daru who had no way of confirming from me and who wanted to see me happy, immediately granted the wish. When I returned to work after the riots had subsided, Mr. Daru called me to his office and congratulated me on the transfer. He told me that he had readily granted my wish of transfer because he wanted to see me content. I got completely confused and asked him what he meant, as I had never requested any such transfer. He explained that D Desai had come to him and made the request on my behalf.

When I exclaimed that I did not wish to be transferred, he said that the transfer orders had been issued and that there was nothing he could do to stop them now. Regional Manager Karnik, who already had a vendetta against me for not being a Marathi, would never let the decision be dissolved. I had no choice in the matter and as upset as I was, I had to start work at the Ulhasnagar branch of the bank. The manager for this branch was Mr. Uchani. I had always been on good terms with him as he would respect me a lot whenever he visited the Regional Office. He was under the supervision of the Deputy Regional Manager, Mr. Mamjeshwar. Uchani wasn't particularly intelligent guy. I felt that he was a rather simpleton, and this was something that bugged Mr. Mamjeshwar a lot. Since Uchani was also very scared of his head, he was bossed and insulted a lot. He wasn't even offered a set in Mr. Mamjeshwar's office. Whenever Uchani visited me, he would cry about this humiliating behavior that he was subjected to, and often stated he would lead the regional head beat him up so that this thing would get out of his system once and for all.

Now that I was working in the same branch as Uchani, it made was very awkward to be with someone whom he used to cry in front of. This made him very bitter. The result was that he would subject me to humiliation and embarrassing situation too often. This, he felt, somehow established his authority over me, as he was my reporting authority. He would find excuses to insult me in front of the staff as many times as he could. But unlike the past me, who would be affected by every little thing that came his way, I was beyond caring about this.

I simply ignored him and even refused to take orders from him, focusing on my day's assigned tasks. This further instigated him, and he would engage in heated arguments with me. I realized quickly that this was not leading anywhere and thereon started answering back to him altogether. This incensed him even more. This new branch in Ulhasnagar housed a staff of more than twenty people, which comprised of the Manager, one Deputy Manager, two officers, including myself, fifteen clerks and two peons. Everyone at work liked me except for the manager, deputy manager, and one girl, who I later found out was a confidante of the manager. I soon became friends with all except these three. They all regarded me highly and would come to me for advice for personal, as well as professional matters. They knew that I was the best qualified in the office and also that I was a humble, quiet person who knew how to keep their secrets.

What's more, I was also a bold person when the situation needed me to be, and this transition in my personality assured them of my strengths. Most of the staff members were Sindhi and would communicate with me in their own Sindhi language. Since I was well versed in written and spoken Sindhi, Punjabi, and Hindi, it was no problem for me to talk to them and understand their issues with ease.

I also understood the Marathi and Gujarati languages well. There were also some young Marathi boys and girls who had taken a fancy to me. They would seek my opinion on their family matters and would even ask my recommendation on movies to watch. Many of them introduced me to their families, and all of them regarded me with high respect. Some parents would invite me to their home for dinner and lunch. I distinctly remember one Marathi Brahmin family who sent me a traditional pure vegetarian meal, with several dishes to accommodate my taste. I have never tasted any food more delicious than the one I had that day. There really is no beating the taste of genuine Marathi food!

Even though there were issues, my work life was going better than I could have hoped for, what with all the grievances that I had to face. I had begun to notice that both the Manager and Deputy Manager were involved in major, corrupt practices that almost everyone at the office knew about but couldn't do much about. All loan applications submitted by clients were handled with extreme secrecy by the manager, deputy manager, and their confidant girl only. No one else was allowed to deal with this side of the bank business.

There were even some large business clients who were granted loans bigger than was in the authority of the branch manager. Customers were asked to clear the loans every Friday for weekly reporting purposes. The next day, they drew the funds again. These business people were contributing huge gifts to the manager and Deputy Manager, along with some secret envelops. I could now see that Manjeshwar, the Deputy Regional Manager, suspected Uchani's malpractices, and this probably was the reason he was so harsh and strict with Uchani. I wasn't really sure what to do in this situation, so I remained quiet. Within two years of my transfer to this branch, Manjeshwar retired. This was a huge relief for Uchani.

Soon after this, I was transferred to another larger branch in Thana, which was about 35 kilometers from my home. Most of the people who worked in this branch of the bank were Marathi and used to look strangely at me. They probably did not expect anyone from any other ethnicity to join them. I got a feeling that most of them thought I was a spy from the head office, which is why they kept a cautious distance from me.

The other thing I noticed immediately was that here, too, all loan portfolios were kept away from everyone except the designated people, the manager, and his confidante loans officer. They would never let me go near any loan documents and prohibited me from talking to any loan customer. I was given the portfolio of deposits and other miscellaneous work. Of course, there wasn't much I could do, so I kept my mouth shut.

It wasn't long before the whole charade started making me uncomfortable, and I started becoming restless. I wanted to get out of this constricting place and do something that was more fulfilling in terms of where my passions lied. So I found a part-time thing in the evening at the Bombay CBD. It was a teaching post in the Indian Institute of Marketing and Management, teaching Costs Management and Industrial Administration to postgraduate students at a senior level.

Most of the students were much older than me, working in senior managerial roles. Some were from the families of wealthy top industrialists. Like before, I was able to retain the love and respect of my students. I was able to convey to them some really tough concepts in a simple and easy to understand manner.

During the same period, I got another teaching position at a top college in Ulhasnagar. It required me to teach costing to senior pharmacy students. At this institute, I met students who were truly brilliant and from high earning families who were into their own businesses or well-paid professional careers. These students, too, loved the way I taught and the fact that I paid attention to their queries and answered them clearly. A new change came in my life at this point in time. I got a proposal from a Sindhi Sikh girl and became engaged to her. You might be interested to know that it was the girl's family who sent the proposal, even though I belonged to a completely different ethnicity. She was two years younger than me and had been in my Sanskrit class when I had been teaching in a high school. I didn't remember her, but she and her family remembered me well.

Her brothers thought that we were a perfect match as they did not care about what cast I was from. They remembered my academics and great achievements. Since the girl, Bhoji, was like me as well, having excelled in her academics, her brothers felt that we were just right for each other. We got married in November 1977 in Ulhasnagar, which was about 60 kilometers from Bombay CBD.

Not many of my bank colleagues attended my marriage, but most of my students from both institutions attended. Soon after getting married, I became even more restless with my bank job. I was desperately in search of something else to do as the work environment in the Bank of India was becoming intolerable for me. I had already spent eight and a half years at the bank and felt that it was a good time to make a shift. I knew that completing the ten years would allow me to get a substantial long service leave, along with provident fund benefits. However, staying at the bank was becoming too much, and I just wanted to get out as soon as possible. Then suddenly, I found what I was looking for. Merely three months after my marriage, in February 1978, I landed the position of a branch manager in the private sector, Oriental Bank of Commerce and Industry, with around a sixty percent raise in the salary. This is where my story at the Oriental Bank begins.

Chapter 5
Corruption Does Not Spare Private Sector My Stint with Oriental Bank of Commerce and Industry Ltd.

Oriental Bank of Commerce and Industry Ltd. (Oriental Bank) was a medium-sized private sector bank that was established in 1943 by the well-known Indian industrialist group, Thapar House. It had more than 200 branches all over the country. In private sector corporations recruitment of staff, particularly for managerial positions, was rarely on merit. Recommendations would select employees from close family members of the top executives and political leaders.

Similarly, promotions would also be by 'recommendations,' and rarely on merit. However, they would religiously follow the process of advertising the positions, then inviting shortlisted candidates for interviews, and then even conduct interviews. Public Sector organizations were not very different, except certain positions required specialized qualifications like Indian

Administrative Services (IAS) and Indian Police Services (IPS). But this was the mindset and practices I detested. I did not believe in using 'source' to get into the right position. Hence the reason why I never used any recommendation and would rely solely on the merit I held. I was truly surprised when my application for the position of Branch Manager was accepted, and I was called for an interview. The Chairman and Managing Directors Mr. M K Vig, General Manager Mr. S P Talwar, Regional Manager Mr. Malhotra and Deputy Regional Manager Mr. Puri, conducted my interview. Chairman Mr. Vig was very impressed with my educational qualifications and varied experience.

He instantly approved me, offered me the position, and started discussing my remuneration. Talwar and Puri felt it was going too fast so they intervened and thanked him for my selection. He was then informed that they will discuss my appointment terms and decide how to move forward with the appointment.

Mr. Vig left the room, and then the remaining three started negotiating the salary package with me. It wasn't long before I realized that Mr. Vig was trying to offer me higher remuneration than the remaining three wanted, which was why they took the matter in their own hands. They ended up offering me only a slightly higher salary against what I was making at the Bank of India, but also made a special allowance of 60% of the salary for my posting as the manager of the Thana branch of the bank. They promised that the special allowance would continue as long as I continued to be a branch manager. I admit that this was my own folly, as I did not see that they were trapping me.

Hence, against all advice from people I knew, I left my secure public sector bank job, refuting my claims on the accumulated leave and provident benefits, and joined the Oriental Bank as Branch Manager of the Thana branch. This too only two months of being married. It was not long before I realized the twisted situation I had gotten myself into. There were little to no customers that came to the Thana Branch, and I was given the responsibility of reviving the dead place to attract more clients and businesses.

I was also told that the previous manager was sacked on the grounds of corruption, as he was giving loans without having the authority to do so. It was later brought to my attention by the staff and a few old customers that this was a lie and the manager was trapped into a game of corruption and deceit by higher authorities. It was, in reality, the 'higher-ups' that were involved in their own nefarious games.

The task that lay ahead of me, though, of reviving the branch was a herculean one, and I could not understand where to begin from. It was a huge challenge, one that I had no idea how to conquer. I had never been a people's person as it was in my personality to be reserved and quiet. But I had to change myself if I was to get the branch to become more active and income generating. So I drastically changed myself, begin to talk more, and communicate the needs of the bank.

With a determined will, I began visiting different businesses in the surrounding areas, simply walking in and introducing myself and my bank. If there was one thing I was sure of, it was that people would never be able to outright say no to the bank manager. Still, it took many months and frequent visits for business owners to start listening to what I had to offer and consider doing business with the Oriental Bank.

There then came a point where my bank was being

talked about, along with the efforts of the manager. I was called the 'dynamic bank manager' as no one before I had made such advances and endeavors. However, I realized that this was not enough; business accounts were not going to cut it. These businesses would expect credit facilities, and I did not have the authority to extend any credit facilities. I desperately needed deposit accounts, but no one was ready to trust the bank with their deposits. A brilliant idea struck me one day as I was looking out the window, deep in thought about what to do to make the bank a more attractive place for depositors. This is when I noticed the school situated right across the road from our bank. It was a large private school, with more than 3000 students. When I tried gaining an appointment with the principal, she refused point blank.

It took a lot of convincing and persistence that eventually allowed for me to pay a visit to her. Once I started meeting her regularly, she soon grew to like and respect me as a qualified branch manager. But she would still not budge about my suggestions of her school opening accounts with our bank.

When I continued to insist on why she was so adamant about not accepting the offer, she told me how they had opened accounts at the bank before on the insistence of my predecessor, but he was abruptly transferred, and the school's banking operations were left orphaned, hanging nowhere. Now, I understood her reluctance in wanting to do business with us. I promised her that this mistake would not be repeated twice, and even if I was transferred, their banking needs would be well taken care of. The principal was still hesitant and did not want to take such a huge financial risk. I decided to try a different tactic and suggested that the parents/students deposit school fees directly at the bank in the school's bank account. This would save them tremendous administrative efforts and costs. In those days, there were no computers, no internet. Every fee check was to be receipted and then manually deposited into their bank accounts.

She instantly liked my proposal and agreed to it happily. Since it was almost the end of the school year, she said they would inform the parents and would start from the upcoming academic year. This was a huge achievement as it meant that now, our bank would attract a lot of people who might consider opening personal accounts with us as well.

New school term started in June 1978, and within a

short span, my bank was filled to the brim with customers queuing to pay school fees. The downside of this was that over the years, the staff of this branch had become lackluster and lethargic. Since the number was also low, it meant hard work for the ones who were currently working there. This created a lot of resistance and resentment among most of them who did not want to work extra hard.

However, they, of course, had no choice as they understood that it was a private bank and they could not refuse direct working orders from the branch manager. If they did not work, they would be thrown out of the bank within the blink of an eye. I had to deal with many tantrums one of which stands particularly well in my memory. There was this one Punjabi female staff, who was related to the bank union leader.

Since she had been working in the bank for 10 years, she felt she could get away with making improper complaints. She told her uncle that I was harassing her and tried to trap me. But I managed to convince the uncle that it was essential that more business be brought to the bank in order to revive its image and show it in a positive light in the community.

Even though he warned me of being careful and never go against his niece or create problems for her in any possible way, he did talk to her and the rest of the staff. He implied the importance of cooperating with me and how it would benefit them all in the long run. He also arranged an additional staff member for my branch. My idea reaped enormous benefits. Soon enough, just as I had predicted and hoped, the same parents who were coming in to submit school fees also opened their personal accounts with my bank. This meant that the once unknown bank branch of Oriental Bank was now pretty famous locally. It had caught the attention of the public and more and more people started coming over and doing business with us. What's more, our publicity grew to the point where we were competing against some large public sector banks and giving them a run for their money! Some of the parents who had opened their accounts in the bank were very senior executives of large corporations, and this meant they were more than happy to bring more business my way.

I had developed a good personal relations with them, and there were quite a few I would honestly call my friends. I would be invited to all their weekend get-togethers, and this allowed me to interact with even more senior executives and form good PR. There were the people who played cards with money. Getting linked to them would mean that I could bring in even more business for my bank.

Whenever I told them to help me out, they were more than willing to send business my way. We were able to procure many business accounts from some very large corporations. Some businesses had substantial turnover, and they required everyday banking transactions, which were numerous and in large quantities. This meant that they would need some temporary credit facility. This was a rather problematic situation for me as I still had not been given the authority to approve any credit facility to my clients, no matter how important they were. This meant I had to refer all such requests to the regional office. Instead of considering the situation, they would never approve any request. They wouldn't even let me have the chance of getting in touch with the chairman. Since I had put in a lot of effort to gain the trust and business of these clients, I did not want to lose them to corruption.

Therefore, I decided to take the risk and accommodate these clients with short term credit without the get-go from higher authorities. I would let them overdraw their bank account for 3-4 days every week with the condition that they would restore their account to credit by Friday, which was my weekly reporting day. I knew this was a huge risk, but I was willing to take it in order to ensure that my clients got their business done smoothly.

Another customer who was the owner of a textile manufacturing and trading business was on the project of trading bills of exchange that were of a substantial amount. I allowed him trading finance by discounting/cashing the bills on Saturday, and the customer would pay back the credit by Friday so that it was not included in the weekly reports. I will not lie and say that I wasn't bestowed with favors, as these two customers did help me with some cash or gifts, but this was not something I paid much heed to. For me, there was no link, nor any relation between the credit facilities I was providing the facilities and the gifts they gave me. After all, these clients had become my friends first. My only purpose and aim was to ensure that the customers remained happy with the bank services so that the bank could maintain the image I had worked so hard to create. Ensuring their happiness also meant retaining their business, which of course would benefit the bank.

Within a year of my joining the Oriental Bank, its business had multiplied by 25 times. Since it was such a huge achievement, the news quickly reached the Chairman, Mr. Vig. He decided to bestow his presence on us at the branch. This was a very rare occurrence as chairmen of banks don't generally visit small branches like ours was. He personally visited me and commended me on all the efforts I had put in making a name for the bank. This had the effect I was afraid of; it made fellow branch managers as well as regional heads envious of me. Hence began another round of trouble that I most definitely could have done without.

Most regional managers could not bear the attention and praise I was getting and decided to attack me in the most vicious way possible. Mr. Puri was the worst and did the most damage. He would put hindrances in my branch's business whenever he thought it would cause disruption in my work and would trace back to me personally. It was also him who started putting ideas in the Regional Manager Mr. Malhotra's mind against me. This was something I grew very upset about because I had a very good working relationship with Mr. Malhotra, who genuinely liked me a lot.

Puri went as far as to appoint an auditor to investigate my branch. When the auditor gave a clean report, Puri doubted the auditor and accused him of corruption, being involved with me, and giving me unduly support. All of these were false accusations, but he refused to listen to any sense. I knew that Puri was constantly hatching plans to discredit me in the eyes of all higher authorities.

He hired an assistant manager to supposedly 'help me' and who was instructed to familiarize with all the major customers I catered to. Within a couple of months, orders for my transfer arrived. I was asked to handover all charge to the assistant manager and was asked to join the regional office immediately. What was even more shocking was that the special allowance that was awarded to me as a branch manager was removed absolutely from my salary. Within a short period, I was reassigned again and was deputed to the Bombay branch as the assistant manager. My special allowance, though, was not restored, and this was simply unacceptable to me. It was insult over injury, and I refused to work for a place that could not respect me for all that I did for them.

Therefore, when the letter of transfer arrived, I refused to report to work and resigned on the spot. Let me assert that this was the point where I had no job prospects in site, but I was still confident that at this point in my career, getting a good job would not be a problem for me. I had, after, all accomplished much, and my success as a branch manager was well known.

I would also like to add that this was the time when my marriage was only three years old. My wife was in an advanced stage of pregnancy, but she did not utter a word against my career choices and resignation. She stood by me stickily and supported everything I did. It is a gesture that I always think of affectionately and with extreme gratefulness. Had it not been for her patience and belief in me, I would never have been able to come as far along as I have so far. She is my pillar, and I want to take out this chance to thank her for all that she has done for our family and me. I would never be able to repay for her trust and faith in me. This was the turning point in my life. It was a phase where even though there was a lot of uncertainty and new developments, I was the surest of myself and my capabilities. I knew that I could do my job well, and this is the reason I refused to let people abuse me or take advantage of me. I was not the stumbling kid anymore who did not know which direction to take or which path to pick.

By this time, I had grown comfortable enough in my skin, as well as my career decisions. I had also learned that getting scared from these corrupt tactics only resulted in damage to myself. This was the reason why resigning from the Oriental Bank was so easy for me. I did not even think twice about it at that moment, nor did I have any regrets over it. I knew it was in my best interest because people like Puri would never let me settle and would continue to attack me from wherever and whenever they could. One more thing that I had learned through this experience was that no matter what happened, even your friends could not be trusted in times of need.

They were only useful to you so long as you were of good use to them. Even though this did not catch me by surprise, it did pang to know that the people you once called friends could actually distance themselves from you in your time of need. In the next chapter of my life, I will talk about how it impacted my life.

Chapter 6
New Beginnings

After leaving Oriental Bank, I decided to take a short break and ponder what it was I wanted to do with my future. The experiences I had there were not something that I wanted to repeat in my next workplace. They had shaken me up more than I cared to admit. The hypocrisy and corruption was one that had left me seething, yet feeling helpless at the same time. There was nothing I could do, yet the injustice of it all rankled me, and I wished to do something to show these corrupt officials that we hard working people, who came from backgrounds different than theirs, did not really need their help or consideration.

I was very regretful of leaving my secure government job. If corruption was everywhere and you could not make an escape from it, then it was better to at least be at a workplace that guaranteed work longevity. I do not blame my luck for all that took place. It was my own blunder that led me to the path of the Oriental Bank. Everyone from my friends to my family had advised me not to leave my job, but I did not pay heed to any of them and faced the worst consequences for that. Leaving the Bank of India's

Ulhasnagar branch was dumb, and I should have known it would cost me a lot. It is one of those regrets that I have to this date. That wasn't the only bad decision I took in terms of my career choice. I completed my all India final exam in Cost and Management Accountancy with a distinction, where I was able to gain the sixth ranking nationwide. Large manufacturing corporations invited me for holding a trainee position. One such corporation was Associated Cement Companies (ACC) that belonged to India's top industrial house of Tatas.

I realized that was perhaps the second chance that Mother Nature was offering me. I readily accepted the invite and agreed to the interview date. However, my best friend Ramesh and my colleagues strongly discouraged me from trying a new private sector job. Foolishly enough, I heeded their stupid advice and skipped the interview. This is another one of the worst blunders I regret to this date. Had I gone to the interview and checked the position out, I may have been able to gain more knowledge and experience than I could have gained from anywhere else. However, I chose to listen to a few foolish people and leave the opportunity of my dreams. Problem was, it wasn't just career difficulties I faced. I had also lost faith in my own capabilities and was unable to generate the same confidence I had before.

It was like I had lost the courage I displayed all my life. The nightmarish experiences with the Bank of India, as well as the Oriental Bank, had affected me in such a bad way that I had lost all sense of confidence. I no longer believed that I could do anything and everything that I put my head to. This meant that applying everywhere became a huge no-no for me.

It was at this point of hesitation and lackluster that I decided to establish my own business. This was something I hadn't thought about getting into, but which made more sense the more I thought about it. So I decided to start a consulting business for different small and medium-sized industrial projects.

I thought such work would use my passion for engineering on the one hand, and my extensive exposure to commercial finance and my multifaceted professional skills acquired through my variegated education on the other hand. I believed it would give me an edge over other people who worked in the same industry. But since I had never done any kind of business, I was rather uncertain about how things would progress. Still, I was willing to take the risk and see how it would work. It was the mid-1980s when I began setting up my own business from a shared tablespace hired by my good friend and well-wisher, Dr. D M Munshi, in the heart of Bombay CBD. He was a very old friend of mine, and I did not only know him, but also his family really well. We were on excellent terms, and I had been to his house dozens of times. He was a doctorate in management and an expert of his field. He was one of those people who knew their work well and had no problem sharing their experience with people less experienced than him. This is the reason I decided to start my business with him, instead of venturing alone.

Since I knew that Dr. Munshi had limited income and that he was struggling to pay the rent for the table, I took responsibility of paying the entire rent for the tablespace and allowed him to share the table with me. He was quite straightforward and honest person for whom I had great respect. He would come to the office only occasionally. Around the same time, I registered a limited liability company in the name of Bee Gee Consultants Pty Ltd, where the B was from my wife's name 'Bhoji' and G from my name 'Gambhir.'

This was the start of a new phase in my life when I begin to turn into a businessman instead of a typical salaried person. Since I respected Dr. Munshi a lot, I wanted to do something to show my appreciation to him. I did this by making him the chairman of my company, even though he had made absolutely no monetary investment, nor had he any kind of shares whatsoever. I think this hit him in all the right places, and he returned the token of appreciation by gifting me an old typewriter that I could use to draft all my proposals. It was one of my most prized possessions, and I took extreme care of this typewriter because it was more than just a tool for me. It was a treasured present from a valuable and esteemed friend and colleague.

Two years of my grilling away in the Oriental Bank, generating business from scratch, gave me the confidence and hope I needed to believe I would be able to generate business from scratch for my own consultancy company. Of course, unlike today, in those days there were no extra means available for marketing techniques. There was no internet, no social media, and nothing that could work when you were short on funds. Since I had little to no money that I could spend on marketing, it meant I had to do everything very creatively and after putting in a lot of thought. So I kept using other measures, which included me going door to door at some times to let businesses know that I was a contender in the market. Through sheer dedication and endless hard work, I was able to expand my business substantially in the next three years. It was an achievement I was truly proud of. I worked like crazy and made a lot of sacrifices to get to where I was. Without trying to sound like I am boasting, most people would have given up had they come across as many difficulties as I had. However, I was determined and passionate, and these two things kept me going, even at times when it seemed like everything would fall apart.

Then something took me by complete shock. The simple looking, highly principled, and honest Dr. Munshi started to make claims that Bee Gee Consultants was his business. I couldn't believe my ears when I heard this the first time. Why would a friend, a mentor, the chairman of my company, make such false claims? I knew that I could counter these false claims very easily and successfully, but I did not want to discredit him and make him my enemy.

I respected and liked him too much for that. So I just tried to have a talk with him and warn him of how wrong he was for making claims like these. Unfortunately, instead of accepting his mistake, he refused to back down. His family members, who used to love me at one point in time, became antagonistic toward me and my family. They even asked me to return the prized typewriter that he had gifted me once he had died. All of this was a serious blow to me, but I had grown accustomed to betrayals and corruption of this kind. So even though I was hurt by this, I did not let it affect me too much. Of course, I won't be justified in taking all the credit for my success and growth. Had it not been for my wonderful wife, I would never have been able to do as well as I was doing. She would encourage me with every new endeavor I became a part of. While I was setting up my business, she had been working as a bank teller/cashier at one of the public sector banks in a branch near our house.

Her income was good enough for us to survive with our basic needs, which included the care for a newly born child, Moksha. When we had gotten married, Bhoji had told me all about how she had dreamt all her life of becoming a doctor, which is why she had taken science in school and college. She had secured high marks in Pre-Professional, two years in college after schooling, but these marks were not enough to get her admission to a medical college to study for medicine so that she could be a doctor in five years. This meant that she needed to donate a huge sum of money, which her parents could not afford. So she then continued her studies in science and completed B.Sc. (Bachelor of Science) with honors, but this too was not enough to get her admission to a medical college without giving substantial donations. She then continued her studies and completed her Masters in Medical Biochemistry, yet was unable to score impressive marks. Thus, her dream of becoming a doctor was finally shattered. It was during her Masters when her family's finances began to deteriorate even more – so much so that it became next to impossible for just one person to work and support the whole family.

Since she had already lost her father at an early age, it was the elder brother (who had been adopted by her parents), who was taking care of the family's finances. He had to take care of the whole family, which included Bhoji, her three younger siblings, and her mother. Since the elder brother had also gotten married and had his own family, it meant that someone else had to work alongside him to make things work well and bear all the finances.

It was at this point that Bhoji had decided to step up and

help her brother out. She felt this was an obligation as she did not wish to become a burden to the elder brother. Her childhood friend, Pushpa, who had been working in a public sector bank, Dena Bank, encouraged her to apply for a position of a cashier at the bank. She did as advised and from then on had been working as a cashier in that bank. This had brought in a lot of ease for the family. When I had first heard Bhoji's sad story, I was surprised that she didn't try to get a job that was relevant to her education. Hence, the reason why I encouraged her to seek a job in line with her profession, so that if she could not be a doctor, at least she could work with them. I could see that she still dreamt of being a doctor, hence the reason I came up with the idea that she should have her very own medical laboratory.

Since she was a Masters in Medical Biochemistry, she would have no difficulty in doing pathological tests. Even though she loved this idea, it was impossible for us to set a lab for her because there was a shortage of funds. But this was something that stuck with me because I knew it would mean the world to my dear wife.

Therefore, when I began my consultancy business, I also started saving money for her laboratory. What we did was we built two rooms annex in front of our house that faced the road. These were built as residences, but it seemed fate had planned something entirely different for us. As it happened, coincidently, one of the clients I was working with had a business of supplying laboratory equipment. He hired me to set up a small-scale factory. As my fees, I asked him to get me a complete set of laboratory equipment at a lower price. This meant that Bhoji now had access to all the equipment she needed to have her medical lab. She was immensely happy and decided to name her lab Bee Gee Pathology. This lab meant that she would not need to travel to work anymore. By this time, we had grown in our finances and had three servants, including a driver. They were all living in servant quarters that was adjacent to the laboratory. I decided that it was time I get Bhoji her very own car. So I invested in a brand new car for her as that would also help her move around with our little baby, Moksha.

The little baby would not have to be away from her mother for longer periods as Bhoji could take her with her wherever she went. As Bhoji had passion for doctors and for her pathology business, she quickly developed a relationship with doctors and hospitals in the local area and neighboring towns. Soon, she became well-known with the doctors and other hospital staff who needed something or the other to do with medical lab services. In this process, she developed a close relationship with one young doctor, which then started affecting our relationship. As I loved my child Moksha so much, and since she loved us both, I could not let her stress about the marital problems that her mother and I were facing. When I had left the Oriental Bank and started my own business, my wife had been almost due for her very first delivery. We were blessed with our very first child on July 16, 1980. She was a beautiful little child who filled my heart with love and satisfaction. It was the most blissful and happy moment of my life. It was so extraordinary and amazing that I had forgotten about all my previous afflictions in its face. Just the thought of becoming a father was enough to fill me up with light. Since my business was very new at that time, I was able to give all my attention and love to the baby girl.

I would spend as much time as possible with her, but with the expanding business, it so happened that I was unable to give her and my family much time. By the time we had our second child, Govinda, born on April 14, 1985, I had become extremely busy with my work and could not spare much time for our newly born son and the family. I continue to regret that I wasn't able to give as much time to my children as I wanted. They deserved to be my first priority, but because of the growing business, I could only spend an hour or two a day with them. Sometimes, even that time was missed out. My hard work paid off, and within a year, I was able to get deals with small and medium industries. This meant I was generating a good income. Since the business was growing every day, I needed to appoint more people to help me out, but due to lack of proper office space, I could not accommodate even a single extra person. The tablespace I had was enough for me, and since my house was far away from my office in Bombay, I could not hire someone to work from my home. I wasn't sure how to solve this issue.

Fortunately, one client, Prem Kumar Khurana, for whom I had arranged a large industrial space and finance for his medical oxygen cylinders project, had big office premises in the posh, newly developed commercial area of Nariman Point. He offered me a big room within his office at a reasonable rent. Hence, I could appoint three employees, and my business continued growing. Prem Kumar had one smaller office on the same floor of the building. When he saw my growing business, he offered me that office for my independent use.

Subsequently, he sold me that office space at a reasonable price, though he had purchased that property for investment purposes, as it had good potential for capital growth. This new office had my personal office room and enough area for the accommodation of staff that was higher than fifteen people at one point in time. I can never forget Prem Kumar Khurana for his selfless act and kindness done to me at a time when I had already been betrayed at the hands of a close friend. It was a huge support as this was the reason that my life changed as my business got an opportunity to grow bigger and better than ever before. His goodwill is something I will always reflect upon with utmost gratitude. Since the beginning of time, all the way back to when I was still a student, I had faced the worst kind of racism and knew what it felt like to suffer under such tyranny. This was the reason I had vowed never to fall prey to these illogical and unfair ideologies. I had promised myself that no matter what happened, I would never make my choices based on a person's cultural and ethnic background and would always appoint my staff purely based on merit.

India has 38 different states, each with a completely

different language and cultural heritage, and with varied sub-castes within each culture. In addition, there are different religious groups in every state – such as Hindus, Sikhs, Muslims, Christians, and Parsis – as well as sub-communities of people from other countries who had made India their home for generations – such as Iranis, Jews, and Portuguese. At one time, I had eighteen staff members each from a different cultural and linguistic background. Of course, all of them would speak and work in English. Then, there are several sub-castes within each culture and of course, the Scheduled Castes – the underprivileged people who were primarily used for low-class manual work (the so-called 'untouchables' – as the higher castes would call them). I refused to ever accept caste, creed, or religion as a reason for discrimination and made sure it was apparent in my business setting.

So long as the person was capable and had the right skills, I was willing to give them a chance to prove their worth. This was perhaps one of the reasons why I have been as successful as I was. It was this work over a period of 12 years that exposed me to all aspects of corruption at a variety of levels. Hence, let us move on to the next chapter to understand the anatomy of corruption.

Chapter 7
Corruption is the Queen in the Westminster Bureaucracy

I had developed the capability to provide all services required to develop an industrial or commercial project from scratch successfully. My brand slogan was 'Concept to Commissioning.' This was way before the modern 'Single Window' concept was conceived. That included organizing all needed government approvals and licenses for the project. In those days, every industrial project needed specific approvals and licenses from several government departments and authorities.

In all honesty, not much has changed in this respect since then. Nonetheless, I understood that people had a difficult time deciphering these things and helping them out would become the way for me to run my business well. This is what I did. I became the connecting line between a layperson and the government officials so that difficult laws could be interpreted easily. Before we proceed further, let us talk about the basic tenets or structure of the Westminster system. At the heart of the system is the concept of the separation of powers between the three branches of government.

- **The Legislature:** This involves the Parliament, which makes the law.
- **The Executive:** This involves the Governor, Prime Minister/Premier, ministers, departments, and agencies, which implement the law made by the parliament.
- **The Judiciary:** This includes the courts, which interpret and apply the law for everyone to follow.

Another key feature of the Westminster System is an apolitical, professional public service, providing impartial advice to the government of the day, and implementing the government's policies and programs. In addition, as it was first proposed in the Northcote-Trevelyan report to the UK House of Commons in 1854, a core requirement of the Westminster system is that the recruitment and promotion of employees in the public service is on the basis of merit. This supposedly meant that people who were appropriate for the job were the only ones who gained it, not those useless people who got in through some kind of bribe or source.

The Ethical Framework for the Government Sector in Australia

Part 2 of the Australian Government Sector Employment Act 2013 establishes the Ethical Framework for the government sector.

Objective

Section 6 of the Act identifies the overarching objective of the Ethical Framework. It is to:

- Recognize the role of the government sector in preserving the public interest, defending public value, and adding professional quality and value to the commitments of the government of the day, and,
- Establish an ethical framework for a merit-based, apolitical, and professional government sector that implements the decisions of the government of the day.

Government Sector Core Values and Principles

Section 7 of the Act identifies the core values and the

principles that guide their implementation.

General Provisions

Section 8 of the Act specifies three general provisions.

- The Public Service Commissioner has the function of promoting and maintaining the government sector core values.
- There is no hierarchy among the core values, and each is of equal importance for everyone.
- Nothing in the framework gives rise to, or can be taken into account in, any civil cause of action.

Secretaries, Heads of Agencies, and Other Senior Executives

Secretaries of Departments (Section 25) and Heads of Public Service Agencies (Section 30) are responsible for the general conduct and management of their organizations in accordance with the government sector core values of the Ethical Framework. Other Senior Executives have similar obligations in their areas of responsibility, as specified in senior executive contracts, work level standards, etc.

Acting in the Public Interest

The objective of the Ethical Framework for the government sector explicitly recognizes the role of the government sector in preserving the public interest. The NSW Ombudsman's Good Conduct and Administrative Practice–Guidelines for State and Local Government provides an important discussion on the nature of public interest, conflicts of interest, and their application by modern public sectors.

The following is a short extract taken from Chapter 3 of this publication.

The Overarching Obligation on Public Officials

Public officials have an overarching obligation to act in the public interest. They must perform their official functions and duties and exercise any discretionary powers, in ways that promote the public interest that is applicable to their official functions.

The Royal Commission addressed this issue into the commercial activities of the government sector in Western

Australia (the 'WA Inc. Royal Commission'). In its report, the WA Inc. Royal Commission said that one of the two fundamental principles and assumptions upon which representative and responsible government is based is:

"The institutions of government and the officials and agencies of government exist for the public, to serve the interests of the public." (Volume 1, chapter 1 at 1.2.5). The Royal Commission noted that this principle (the 'trust principle') "expresses the condition upon which power is given to the institutions of government, and to officials, elected and appointed alike." Later in its report it noted that [g]overnment is constitutionally obliged to act in the public interest" (Volume 1, Chapter 3 at 3.1.5).

The Components of the Public Interest

Acting in the public interest has two separate components:

Objectives and Outcomes: The objectives and outcomes of the decision-making process are in the public interest.

Process and Procedure: The process adopted and the procedures followed by decision-makers in exercising their discretionary powers are in the public interest, which includes the following:

- Complying with applicable law (both in terms of letter and spirit).
- Carrying out functions fairly and impartially, with integrity and professionalism.
- Complying with the principles of procedural fairness and/or natural justice
- Acting reasonably, no matter what personal thoughts or feelings might be.
- Ensuring proper accountability and transparency.
- Exposing corrupt conduct or serious maladministration, no matter who they may be.
- Avoiding or properly managing situations where their interests might reasonably be perceived to conflict with the impartial fulfillment of their official duties.
- Acting apolitically in the performance of their official functions (not applicable to elected public officials).

What Does 'Public Interest' Mean?

It is important to draw a distinction between the

question and its application – between what 'is' the public interest and what is 'in' the public interest in any particular circumstance. Perhaps this difference is what allows so many officials to create discrepancies and generate benefits for themselves, which may otherwise not be in the benefit of the public or masses. Hence, this is the reason why corruption is at such a high, no matter what country you belong to. The only difference I see and feel is that in some places like Australia, it is caught. While in other places, like India, it goes or is let go unnoticed.

What is Not in the Public Interest?

In some ways, it is easier to distinguish the public interest from what it is not. For example, the 'public interest' can be distinguished from:

Private Interest: These are the interest of a particular individual or individuals, although there are certain private 'rights' viewed as being in the public interest.

Personal Interest: These are the interest of the decision-makers, including the interests of members of their direct families, relatives, business associates, etc. Public officials must always act in the public interest ahead of their personal interests and must avoid situations where their private interests conflict, may potentially conflict, or may reasonably be seen to conflict with the impartial fulfillment of their official duties.

Personal Curiosity: It can be referred to what is of interest to know which gratifies curiosity or merely provides information or amusement to be distinguished from something that is of interest to the public, in general.

Personal Opinion: These are, for example, the political or philosophical views of the decision-maker, or considerations of friendship or enmity.

Parochial Interests These are the interests of a small or narrowly defined group of people with whom the decision-maker shares an interest or concern.

Partisan Political Interests These are, for example, the avoidance of political/government or agency embarrassment. These can be categorized as motivation-type issues that focus on the private, personal, or partisan interests of the decision-maker, and possibly also those of third parties.

What is 'The Public Interest?'

'The public interest' is best seen as the objective of, or

the approach to be adopted in, decision-making rather than a specific and immutable outcome to be achieved. The meaning of the term or the approach indicated by the use of the term is to direct consideration and action away from private, personal, parochial, or partisan interests, towards the matters of broader, i.e. more 'public' concern.

While the meaning of 'the public interest' stays the same, the answer to the question of what is 'in' the public interest depends almost entirely on the circumstances in which the problem arises. It is this variable content which makes the term useful as a guide for decision-makers.

For further information from the NSW Ombudsman on how to act in the public interest, the following resources are available.

- Good Conduct and Administrative Practice: Guidelines for state and local government (2nd edition), NSW Ombudsman: www.ombo.nsw.gov.au/__data/assets/pdf_file/0016/3634/Good-Conduct-2nd-edition-amended.pdf.
- Chris Wheeler, Deputy Ombudsman, 'The public interest revisited — we know it's important but do we know what it means?' in Australian Institute of

Administrative Law Forum, No. 72, March 2013, at page 34: www.aial.org.au/Publications/webdocuments/Forums/Forum72.pdf.

- How do public interest considerations impact the role of public sector lawyers? Presentation to the Public Sector In-House Counsel Conference Canberra, 30-31 July 2012, by Chris Wheeler, Deputy Ombudsman: www.ombo.nsw.gov.au/__data/assets/pdf_file/0019/8065/Public-interest-Presentation-How-do-public-interest-considerations-impact-Public-Sector-In-House-Counsel-Conference-Canberra-30-July-2012.pdf.
- Public interest factsheet, NSW Ombudsman: www.ombo.nsw.gov.au/__data/assets/pdf_file/0014/3713/FS_PSA_16_Public_interest.pdf.

Some countries that come under the Westminster system are:

- Australia
- Barbados
- Canada

- Commonwealth of Dominica
- Guyana
- India
- Republic of Ireland
- Jamaica
- Malaysia
- Malta
- New Zealand
- Singapore
- The Republic of South Africa (partially)
- Trinidad and Tobago
- The United Kingdom

Here lie the traps for the common man who can never decipher anything from these legal provisions and regulations. The bureaucrats (public servants) develop a set of regulations, procedures, forms, and documentation for every set of activity to be performed by them for the benefit of the general public and public interest.

No single level of bureaucracy has complete authority to one major task. Hence, the process of authorizations and approvals travels through a series of authorities. However, in practice, there are delegations given by a higher authority to the lower authority with limitations and pre-conditions. This is where the system of extensive paperwork and documentation is involved to satisfy the conditions and requirements. It could be very cumbersome and painful for an ordinary person to go through this paperwork in which only the relevant public sector officials have the expertise. They are the only person who can guide and/or assist an ordinary person (applicant of a relevant approval or license). But the employer public sector agency does not give any extra remuneration for giving such advice or assistance as it is their standard job requirement to do so.

Hence, there exists corruption in the form of incentives to be provided by the applicant. As a consultant offering my clients all services from ‘concept to commissioning,’ it was my responsibility to deal with the public sector officials. I will share my deep-level experiences in the next chapters of this book.

Chanakya Neeti (Policy)

Much earlier than the conception of the Westminster system, Bharat Varsh or India had an advanced administration system. Chanakya is considered the father of that system. Chanakya, also known as Kautilya and Vishnu Gupta, is one of the most influential figures in Indian history. He was the brains behind the brawn of Chandragupta Maurya, who successfully upended the Nanda Dynasty and laid the foundation of the Maurya Empire, which under his successors, Bindusara and Ashoka, became the first and the largest empire in India. It was only matched – but not exceeded – later on only by the Mughal Empire and Gupta Empire, as well as to a certain extent by the Chola dynasty.

Apart from being a royal adviser, Chanakya was also a teacher, economist, philosopher, and jurist. He even wrote Arthashastra – one of the most revered political treatises in India.

The Major Sayings of Chanakya

Chanakya touched a wide variety of issues in Arthashastra. He is also held as a major predecessor of classical economics. Here are a few of his points that stand out. They may be enumerated as below.

- It is always important to learn from the mistakes that others make, since life is too short to make all mistakes by yourself and then learn from them.

- It is always important to be a good person since the goodness of an individual is all pervasive. It can be felt anywhere and everywhere.
- It is not always in one's interest to be completely honest since honest people often face problems.
- There is no God in statues and idols. The soul is the temple of a human being, and his or her emotions are the God.
- Even if someone does not have the means, he or she should behave like he or she has them nonetheless.
- It is deeds that make someone great, and not the family where he or she was born into.
- There is no friendship where there is absolutely zero self-interest. It may be hard to accept this, but it is a fact.
- It is always important to make friends with people of a similar stature since friendships with ones below or above you will never make you happy.
- It is always important to be clear about a few things before one does any work. You should know your reasons for doing some thing, its results, and possibilities of success. Only after deep thought and proper answers should one undertake a task.

- It is always important to treat kids in the first five years of their lives like absolute darlings and keep reprimanding them for all their mistakes in the next decade of their lives. However, when they turn 16-year-old, they should be regarded as friends since children who have grown up can be the best friends for parents.
- It is always important to attack and destroy any source of fear in sight.
- Just like a visually-impaired or challenged person has no use for a mirror, a stupid individual can derive nothing from a book.
- The beauty and youth that a lady possesses is the most important power in the world.
- Education is always the best friend of an individual. It is something that helps one be respected universally and wields greater power than virtues such as youth and beauty.
- It is always important to be wholeheartedly dedicated to any work and not worry about failures since sincere people happen to be the happiest as well.

Chanakya's Views on Success and Leadership

Chanakya says that success never happens accidentally. It happens only when the person is properly focused and is able to align this virtue with actions that have a lot of thoughts behind them. He also says that for a leader, it is important to be fearless, persevering, and patient. These qualities help one set goals, which would otherwise be regarded as too high. Such qualities help the leader formulate proper plans and execute them well. A leader should also be good enough to identify talent and groom them properly so that they are able to take on bigger challenges in life.

Why are These Views Important in Today's World?

Chanakya's thoughts have been revered highly for generations in India, and not without reason. His thoughts and sayings are universal and can be applied to every sphere of one's life, as well as in the public space. He prescribes balance in personal life, while emphasizing areas such as importance of education and qualities such as success and leadership. More than anything, these are perhaps the best motivational tools that one can access in this day and age.

Chanakya suggested a three-step process to convince someone to make them do what you want.

- Diplomacy, by peaceful persuasion with requests, love-filled talk with patience, and emotional blackmail.
- If that does not work, then offer some cash or in-kind incentives to do the work.
- If even that does not work, then do it with force, including brutal force and torture.

You can see that the second step is nothing but corruption. Indian bureaucrats had the advantage of the best of both worlds to learn from and practice corruption for their personal benefits. It is without doubt that we can deduce its source. This is where they learned corruption from. The second and third points clearly state that people should take other measures if their stance is not accepted.

This is where a flawed ideology takes place that ultimately leads to corruptions, not only in our personal lives, but also in our professional ones. What I have understood and we as a nation need to understand is that these roots of corruption run too deep to end easily. There is a need for re-educating the masses. People need to be taught from the very start the values that are necessary for ethical purposes. I have noticed from school that children take their inspiration from the adults, which means that if adults do something wrong, then children follow suit. This is where teachers come into the picture. Teachers need to be of the best emobiment of ethics. Their students would learn from them and follow their example for all time to come. This is something I understood since my childhood and something that I tried to practice in my daily life at all times. This was the reason I insured that my practices were moral with the aim of reducing any kind of corruption. I knew that people were used to getting bad treatment from everyone, which was why I tried to be the different one. I wanted to create a difference. I wanted to bring a change to the way officials were perceived, by helping people out, and not taking advantage of their difficulties.

Unfortunately, this was a monstrous task and I saw that things were not easy for me simply because I had decided to change the country I worked and lived in. No matter where I went, corruption seemed to follow suit. This is why it was tough for me to work either in the public or private sector. Even when I tried my hand at my own business, I came across people who only made things tougher for me. In the upcoming chapters, I will narrate my tale of how things progressed for me in Australia, what were the differences, and what were the similarities in the working sector of Australia and India. It will help you see how countries, their laws, and people make a difference, and how you can assimilate into various systems.

Chapter 8
The Corruption in Action

Every industrial unit requires land with basic infrastructure and amenities such as electricity, water, and council facilities. The process of organizing these basic things requires immense resources and funds, as well as a long time in obtaining the requisite statutory approvals. Only larger corporations with unrestricted resources and manpower can afford this luxury. Small and medium sized industries can never venture into this 'adventure.'

The Indian government has perhaps one of the world's best five-year-plan systems, which is operated and controlled by a special authority called the Planning Commission since 1950s. This Planning Commission is chaired by the Prime Minister. Industrial growth at all levels is one of the top priorities under this planning system.

Back then, every state was asked to set up Industrial Development Corporation whose prime responsibility was to acquire large piece of lands, mostly in the rural areas close to major cities, and arrange all the required infrastructure. Such land was then divided into small parcels of say in multiples of 1000 square meters and leased on long-term (99 years) basis at a lump sum price determined by the expert committee of the corporation. The small and medium industrial units would be allotted land as per their requirement as expressed in their respective business plan. The process of application seemed simple, but in practice it was quite complex as several documents and plans were required to be submitted when demanded by the related officials of the State Industrial Corporation. This generated goldmines of corruption for the public servants at all levels. How? Simply because the layman could not easily decipher what was asked of them and the officials took full advantage of this.

My office was in Bombay, which comes in the Maharashtra State. My initial concentration was there and in the surrounding areas of the state. I therefore had to deal with the Maharashtra Industrial Development Corporation (MIDC) for clients' needs. Acquiring appropriate land for my clients was a major initial job of my consultancy assignment. I started visiting the Bombay headquarters of MIDC and learned about their procedures and documentary requirements. Until then, I was naïve in the field of corruption.

Yes, I had experienced it a lot, but that most certainly did not mean that I was proficient in identifying or doing it myself. I had no idea how to identify the right person in the MIDC for a project as there were several officials involved at different levels for each industrial area. Due to my experience at the banks, I directly established rapport with the chief executive officer/managing director. He soon became friends with me and praised my work for helping foster industrial projects. But he never committed directly supporting any one project application. He would say that the proper procedure needed to be followed and would refer me to the relevant official.

This was the same as what ordinary citizens had to experience. We did not know our rights and could not truly understand the system, hence the gullibility prevailed. The lower officials welcomed me, but neither helped nor guided me in any possible way. They suggested submitting the application with all listed documents, which would be put in the queue with other applications. The lower officials would then pretend to be extremely busy, like they were overloaded with applications. They would state that they would start processing my application when its turn came.

That turn, of course, never came on its own.

This was something that I could not make do with, as this much time would eventually mean that I would lose the client to delays and incompetence. After some weeks, I befriended a consultant whom I would see in the MIDC office. As much as I dislike to confess this, he was the kind soul who was nice enough to guide me toward my first step in corruption. He very well knew the concerned MIDC official name Mr. A. B. Rahate and suggested that I put some cash in an envelope and walk into his office, even if someone is already with him, and put the envelop into his table drawer.

This was my first lesson in bribery and corruption. I have to admit that it made me extremely uneasy and reminded me that I wanted to be above this. But this was the time which also showed me clearly that if I wanted to get any official work in time, I had no choice but to adhere to the rules of corruption. I hesitantly followed his instructions and did exactly what was suggested to me. When I did not get any response or reaction from Rahate, I waited for some moments.

Then, to my amusing surprise, he said, *"I know it is*

there."

I found those words very amusing and still remember that incident. That was my induction to the school of corruption. Even though I was amused by the whole event, it taught me a lesson for life. *If you want to get government work approved in time, bribe the official in charge.* Suffice it to say that India was not the only place where I experienced this thing – that is a tale for later chapters.

After this, my life became easier. I went on successfully completing several projects in every corner of the State of Maharashtra. I made good acquaintances with resourceful entrepreneurs, who promoted me among their friends. My experiences taught me exactly who the right people were, what kind of friendships I could form with them, how they could aid me, what kind of bribery worked for whom, and whether there was anyone who was truly loyal to me.

I have to stress again that this corruption did not sit easy with me and I was almost always stressed about what I had fallen into. But as I said before, it was not something I had control over either, nor was it something I could change. If I wanted to run a successful business, I would need to work with these people on their terms, not my own. My business multiplied faster with the word of mouth from my satisfied clients. Prem Kumar Khurana, my savior, who offered me his precious commercial premises for my business, also introduced me to one of my most satisfied and highly impressed clients, Baldev Sahney. I did projects in other states too, such as Gujarat, neighboring Maharashtra, Punjab, and Uttar Pradesh in northern India. Gujarat Industries and Investment Corporation (GIIC) is perhaps the most efficient government body in all of India. I did some excellent projects in Gujarat without much hassle.

When it comes to UPSIDC, I had truly unique experiences there as the staff was very lethargic and callous. I would have appointments with its managing director at 11:30 a.m. and I would always reach there in time, thinking that since he held the highest position in the organization, he would prefer discipline and timeliness from his guests. But I ended up receiving a shock for my false assumptions.

Here is what happened. It was an over two-hour long flight from Bombay. When I reached his office, even his secretary had not arrived, and other staff had no information of my appointment or my desire to meet their head. When I mentioned that his secretary had fixed his meeting with me at 11:30 a.m., everyone started laughing as if I had cracked a joke. They informed me that he never came to the office before 2:00 p.m. and also said that I must be from outside because everyone locally knew that his 11:30 a.m. meant 2:30 p.m. and would come accordingly for the appointment. It was him who had invited me to discuss how I could bring agro-industrial projects to his state, yet this lack of interest persisted. I am pretty sure that by now, you would have an idea of what the officials, even the highest ones of the order, were like. They simply did not respect anyone, nor did they care about the decorum of their position. Corruption had increased to the point where wrong was not even believed to be wrong and there was no one who had the thought or vision to raise their voices against it.

So what could I do in such a system? Adhere to what was law and keep my conscience at an all-time low. By this time, I was attending several conferences on management, as well as industry-specific topics such as packaging and food processing, small-scale engineering projects, etc. This made me known in several professional and industrial sectors. I had made presentations and written papers on how to save wastage of agro produce, such as potatoes and fruits, which would be rotting due to a lack of transportation. I suggested suitable industrial projects for processing such agricultural products that would be otherwise wasted. This earned me a good reputation in the market.

The managing director of the Punjab State Industrial and Development Corporation (PSIDC) invited me to discuss a large food processing and packaging project in which a large industrial house known as Oswal was also interested. I was told that it would be a joint venture between the PSIDC and Oswal Group. When I arrived for the meeting, the MD and Abhey Oswal were present together with their senior staff. I was profusely welcomed, and my ideas were appreciated.

After discussions throughout the day, I was invited to join them for the dinner. It was agreed that we would meet again after two weeks in the office of Abhey Oswal. But like so many times before, when my fate seemed not to work in my favor, things did not go as planned. Unfortunately, soon thereafter, the Oswal group split as the brothers were fighting for control of the group. My project was shelved in this family feud, and I was left disappointed.

This most certainly was a setback, but nothing that I had not experienced before. I was used to such disappointments and had learned not to let them get to me. Life had taught me that no matter what the situation, things do not stay the same and eventually come to fruition one way or the other. So failure was not something that held me back and I taught myself to get back on my feet after continuing to fall down repeatedly. And this is what I did that time, too. So far, I have talked about only one basic need for an industrial project – land with infrastructure. Another major need of an industrial project is the long-term financial investment at low interest rates, which was very scarce and very difficult to secure. Traditional banks would finance only large industrial projects of well-known industrial houses. The Indian government had issued mandatory directions to all the public sector banks to extend 20% of their total loans to priority sector.

Small-scale industries were included in the priority sector. But banks hesitated to provide long-term loans to these priority sector units. They just focused on the working capital needs of the small-scale industrial units. Every state was asked to set up financial corporation to extend long-term loans to the small and medium scale industrial units to meet their initial capital requirement. Maharashtra had Maharashtra State Financial Corporation (MSFC) for small-scale industries and State Industrial Investment Corporation of Maharashtra (SIICOM) for medium-scale industries. Here lied another goldmine for corruption on which I will talk about in the next chapter. It was, and still is, the state government's documented policy that the chief executive and all the senior executives and officials must be hired from local ethnic people of the state. In Maharashtra, ethnic people were Marathi speaking and heritage Maharashtrians. When I was born, there was no Maharashtra State – it was rather the Bombay Presidency. In 1960, the then Indian Prime Minister created linguistic-based states. The Bombay Presidency was split into two newly created states – Maharashtra and Gujarat. Though I was born prior to the birth of Maharashtra, I did not fall into the ethnic Marathis, and this inevitably became a problem for me.

This happened to me at the Bombay University. The University of Mumbai, known earlier as University of Bombay, is one of the earliest state universities in India and the oldest in Maharashtra. I completed three degrees in the years 1966 to 1976 – Bachelor of Advanced Economics and Applied Statistics, Bachelor of Commerce, and Master of Commerce. In 1992, I needed transcripts of these degrees for Australian Visa purposes. In those days, everything was done manually, which made room for corruption. I was told that it would take three months as they had to dig old records stored in archives and that required a series of authorizations. I could not afford that long a wait and therefore requested urgent attention.

The official told me if I would be a Maharashtrian, I could get priority and that he could arrange it within six weeks. He refused to accept me as a Maharashtrian, even with my argument that I was born there before the Maharashtra was born. Finally, seeing my desperation, the official suggested that if I was willing to spend cash, then I could get everything I needed within ten days. I had no alternative, but to go that route. I paid 50 percent of the agreed amount in advance and balance upon collection of my transcript.

Maharashtrians, like other ethnicities in every state, are highly racist. But, as the old English saying goes, 'Money makes the mare go.' They too would be willing to do anything when they were paid the right amount for it. I experienced the same countless times during my time in

Maharashtra.

They say music has no language – that it has its own unique language which appeals to everyone. The same is said for love. I add corruption to this category as well. Corruption cannot be racist. It has its own unique universal race which does not distinguish anyone. It only sees the color of money and loves all colors, so long as the color of money is paid. You may be interested to know that this is not only true for the people of Maharashtra. It is rather universal. People of all race and color prefer the color of money to everything else, which means that so long as you have the currency to show, you will be respected, you will be welcomed, and you will be given your due course. I learned this the hard way, but it was not something that I could escape. If I wanted any job done, be it for personal reasons or professional ones, I would have to give in to this system of corruption and bribery.

Only when I paid the officials their due money were they willing to even look at the job I needed done. Like I mentioned before, I detested this thing and wanted to stay above it all, but it was impossible. So I learned to cope and make do with what I had at hand. What I did was make sure that I did not fall into this trap where people would find the need to bribe me or lure me personally into corruption.

What's more? I always insured that I was above the whole 'ethnicity favoritism' as I like to call it. For me, all humans were equal, no matter what color or creed they came from. I treated them the same. I admit that this caused me to fall in a lot of problems from time to time, but it also worked in my favor, as people did not only like me for my fairness, but they also trusted me with personal information. They knew that no matter what, I would not betray their trust or cause them any kind of harm. Perhaps, this was one of the reasons why I was able to expand my business quickly and surely. People trusted me not only for the work I did, but also for my ethics and promise. I would meet their expectations and go further beyond.

In the next few chapters, I will tell you how this honesty and sincerity of mine helped and caused damage to my life as well. I faced severe losses in both personal and professional lives but they taught me lessons that made me the man I am today. I have experienced a world of experiences and come across some of the worst and the best people this place has to offer. If there is one thing I am proud of, it is my ability to adapt and find the best in all kinds of situations. I hope through this book of mine, you will find guidance.

Chapter 9
Survival of the Corrupt

The functioning of the state financial corporations was no different than that of the state industrial development corporations. Whatever is the situation, the 'corruption' remains the Queen everywhere, no matter what part of the world you are in. In the past, my preference was to establish direct contact with the chief executive officer of each of the two state financial corporations MSFC and SIICOM. Out of the two, it was relatively easier to establish a working relationship with the managing director of MSFC, Mr. Ranade.

Dr. Munshi had taught him in management school, so I already knew something about him. He was a nice gentleman, soft-spoken, and humble person. He was inspiring and cooperative and encouraged me to take my clients to MSFC. But I had to start with the lower officials who would process my applications and present my requirements to the MD for final approval. I had to prepare a detailed project feasibility report to accompany the applications I would send in. The small-scale entrepreneurs did not know how complex it was to prepare a project feasibility report. I had to engage external engineering technocrats at a fee. My clients did not see the value of preparing the project feasibility reports because they did not understand its importance. For them, it was just another document in the routine paperwork so that they did not pay any extra charges. I would have to be the one to cover all my costs myself, without any kind of aid from the clients, including the pre-agreed, highly negotiated fees.

Of course, the bribe or corruption money had to be paid as well to the officials at MSFC, without which they would not even bother to progress my application at all. I already explained in the previous chapter how it was impossible to get any official work done without some kind of bribe paid to even the lowliest of officials.

By this time, I had gotten used to handling corruption as a part of my work routine. This was because I had accepted that there was little to nothing that could be done without bribes and pleasing people. This gave me a hard time, but there was nothing I could do, and I had realized early on that if I wanted a business that worked, I would need to work like the people who were already a part of that industry. Hence, I had removed any preconceived notions and learned to do as required by the setting and time.

SIICOM was the place where it was most difficult to establish contacts. Its managing director, Mr. Rajendra Gharse, was a tough cookie to crack. I would suspect any new person, especially the one not speaking Marathi, being a spy. It took a long time to win his trust. His rate of corruption was high. Like a shrewd businessman, he would decipher what my advantage in the deal was and then accordingly demand a share of it instead of taking a consistent rate every time.

However, once a deal was in place, he would go out of the way to help with any difficult situation. Although it took a long time to establish a satisfactory working relationship with him, as soon as a conclusion was attained, it became much easier to land every new application in just the right office, and everything was handled like a classic business deal.

In one of the conferences on industrial development, I stumbled across Prem Kumar Gupta of Laxmi Ratan Engineering Group, an established industrialist who had large textile mills and textile engineering industries. He was very impressed with me and my professionalism. Over some time, we became good friends. He would regularly visit my office or invite me to his office – a large place in an elegant sandstone heritage building He would also invite me to his industrial units, and even his house – an elegant large bungalow in Pedder Road. This was Bombay's most expensive and posh residential area where every resident was an industrialist or a top executive of a large public sector corporation. He was given the accommodation as a part of his remuneration package.

Prem Kumar was a very simple, humble, and honest man, unlike most businesspeople. He was going through a rough time when we became acquaintances. His large textile mill in the heart of Bombay was being closed due to militant workers' union actions. He introduced me to his longtime (over 35 years) personal secretary and advisor, Mr. Khattar, who seemed like his great supporter.

Prem Kumar requested me to work with Khattar to solve his problems. Soon I observed that Khattar was a dishonest man and was siphoning money off the company for his benefits. With that money, he had purchased a large apartment in Nepean Sea Road area – another posh and expensive area. Now, this was something I couldn't solve callously and had to handle the situation delicately and carefully. I think Khattar could sense that I knew about his dishonesty.

Hence, soon he resigned. For Prem Kumar, it came as a relief as he was saved from spending a large amount every month on this white elephant. His problems were too big, and he knew this very well, but he managed to remain calm and composed throughout his ordeal. Khattar reminded me of another dishonest and thankless person called Mehta whom I met during my tenure as a branch manager at Oriental Bank. Mehta was a longtime private secretary of Kamani, the well-known owner of Kamani Group of Industries.

Kamani's industrial unit in Thana was in trouble, and he was desperately looking for capital. That was a great opportunity for my bank branch – a big industrial group willing to shift its banking transactions to my bank branch. Mr. Kamani personally visited my branch, which was rare for an industrialist of his stature. Most businesspeople would always send their assistants to banks.

However, as usual, my regional office did not support me. That aside, after the first visit by Kamani, Mehta was delegated to deal with me. Within our initial dealings, I observed Mehta's dishonesty. He did not hesitate even once before suggesting that I should ask a huge cash incentive from Kamani in return for the work my bank would do for him. Mehta would then share the amount equally with me. I was shocked, so I refused to do any such thing. Things got sour between Mehta and me. He could not believe I had refused such an offer and hence made things as difficult for me as he possibly could. My friendship with Prem Kumar Gupta flourished. He developed a lot of respect for me. He introduced me to his son-in-law, Badal Mittal of Mittal Group – who had built several multistory high-rise buildings at Nariman Point and other affluent districts of Bombay.

He also introduced me to his younger brother, Pushpa Kumar Gupta, who was married to the sister of Dr. B. K. Modi of the House of Modis, another large industrial group. Pushpa Kumar had his small industrial unit on the outskirts of Delhi and was looking to start a new medium-sized industrial unit, preferably with foreign collaboration, with a limited investment of his own.

My turnkey assignment included providing everything for setting his project, starting with researching and shortlisting project ideas. I had done substantial research on the line of packaging of all types. Therefore, I started working with my researched and shortlisted projects in this field without any difficulty whatsoever. This was my entry into the high and mighty of the society that was affluent and filthy rich. I came across another project idea for the manufacturing of 200-liter H. M. Polymer drums with rings like the steel drums that would exclusively be used by large petroleum companies for retail-selling liquid petroleum products. Pushpa Kumar readily accepted my project idea and asked me to proceed. We signed a contract under which I had to acquire technical collaboration and plant equipment from an international source as there was no company in India that provided technology and manufacturing plants for the project. Eventually, I had to start with land acquisition, appointing engineers for building and so on – including the arrangement of finances and all other resources required until the commencement of production.

I organized technical collaboration using supplies and the installation of the entire plant and equipment with a reputed German company, Mauser. I simultaneously arranged land from MIDC in a prime industrial zone near Bombay. Pushpa Kumar and I finalized the building contract with a reputed company that I had introduced. The basic building and plant layout were supplied by Mauser. Long-term capital finance was organized by ICICI, while working capital and importation facilities were provided by the State Bank of India.

Once the project had made substantial progress, we decided to raise additional funds by issuing shares to the general public through an IPO. As Pushpa Kumar Gupta was an unknown entity, we asked his wife's brother, Dr. B. K. Modi of Modi House of Industries, to be the chairman of the company. Dr. Modi was highly reputed and an influential name in the investment market and in the eyes of the general public. I handled the entire process of IPO, including organizing the required underwriting of IPO, press conferences, and nationwide meetings with the share and stockbroking groups in every major city.

This all went extremely well, and it was an exciting and educating experience for me. In every major press conference and brokers meeting, I would be sitting between Dr. B. K. Modi on my right and Pushpa Kumar on my left. This was because I had a complete grip on every aspect of the project. Dr. B. K. Modi would answer all the questions. I would readily respond and instantly pass my notes to him. He was very impressed with my efficiency and diligence. Eventually, he expressed his desire that I work for him and his group of companies.

But Pushpa Kumar did not want to lose me. He offered me the position of chief executive officer of the new company, Presti-Mauser HM Poly Containers Limited, on the condition that I did not provide my services to his elder brother Prem Kumar Gupta, who had introduced Pushpa Kumar to me with strong pleas to help them in any way I could. I had already discovered that Pushpa Kumar was a dishonest and disloyal person, especially toward his elder brother, but I had never imagined that he would stoop to such a low level. Of course, I would never accept that condition, so I refused his offer on the spot.

It was sickening to see that the elder brother was so concerned about the younger one, but all the younger brother wanted to do was cause financial harm to his loving elder brother. I could not imagine how much deceit and malice resided in Pushpa Kumar's heart for such things to fester. Even though I was disgusted with this, I still had to work alongside him because of our ongoing project. Our reputations were at stake. The IPO was successful and oversubscribed multiple times. Later, when the project was near completion, and it was time for the payment of my agreed fees of Indian Rupees 1.50 million (which was then equivalent to US$ 150,000), Pushpa Kumar re-negotiated my agreed fees as per the signed contract. He said that my fee of $150,000 was too much and that he would pay me only $60,000. That was my first large successful project, which had been diligently completed. Since I had high regards for his elder brother, Prem Kumar, I did not challenge the contract and accepted the reduced fee.

Pushpa Kumar then started haggling with the building contractor, Mohan Makhija, who had, at my assurance, completed the factory building with partial payment on the verbal guarantee that the balance would be paid from the proceeds of the IPO. Pushpa Kumar refused to pay him his full amount and the matter had to go for litigation in the Bombay High Court.

Pushpa Kumar was not bothered as he turned out to be a seasoned cheater and already knew that the court would take years. This was another setback that I experienced from the corrupt people of the world. Even though all his work had gone better than could have been expected, this attitude was unsettling. Luckily, life has a way of coming back and giving you back what you plant for others. He got it tit for tat. He leased office space across the road from my office and appointed a person, referred to him by his wife through Modi House, as CEO.

Soon this person siphoned huge amount of cash off the company, and eventually, the company went bankrupt. This was something that Pushpa deserved, not only because of his dishonesty with me, but also for his disloyalty to his elder brother. He was not honest himself and therefore only attracted corruption his way, too, in the form of people who were working for him. I, on the other hand, was doing well. My business was flourishing, and I was expecting larger industrial projects whose financial needs were beyond the lending capacity of SIICOM. I, therefore, had to look for national-level financial corporations and large public sector banks.

I established a working relationship with ICICI (Industrial Credit and Investments Corporation of India), IDBI (Industrial Development Bank of India), India's largest bank, State Bank of India (owned by the government since its inception prior to the nationalization of fourteen major banks), Canara Bank, Bank of Baroda, Union Bank, and others. The chairman and managing director (CMD) of State Bank of India (India's largest bank), Dr. A. K. Bhattacharya, introduced to me by Badal Mittal (Prem Kumar Gupta's son-in-law), was impressed with me, and soon became a good friend of mine.

He helped me a lot with my clients' projects without expecting anything from me in return. Another person who had a good impression of me was Mr. S. P. Pai, CMD of Canara Bank (another government-owned bank). He also became a good friend of mine, but never helped me with any of my client projects. Every time, he would make promises and put me in the process, but these would never come to fruition. He behaved as if he was an honest, humble person and never even spoke about corruption in the bank. However, I later found out that he was an extremely corrupt man and would never do any work without receiving a hefty amount. Hence, I did not dare to take a chance with him by offering him any amount.

I can never forget the plight of Prem Kumar Gupta at the hands of his sons and wife. I first met him at his head office in Fort, Bombay. His office room was high and spacious, decorated with rich mahogany and teak wood furniture and huge leather sofa with leather chairs. One had to take an appointment a week in advance to meet him. When I had met him, he took an instant liking to me, and we would meet both professionally, as well as personally. After that, he used to invite me to his large textile mill in the Bombay industrial area about 10-12 kilometers from Bombay CBD. The mill employed over 2,500 workers. Then, we met at another large textile engineering factory about 35 kilometers from Bombay CBD. His big bungalow was situated in the most influential residential area. He introduced me to his two young sons, who had recently graduated, and asked me to help set up a new modern industrial project of a decent size – preferably with foreign technology/collaboration for them. Since they did not take an interest in the family business of textile and engineering, Prem Kumar wanted to insure they had a livelihood of their own that they took enthusiasm in.

Within three to four years, Prem Kumar's business and financial situation deteriorated drastically, mainly due to the militant and destructive labor union. His two sons, Amit and Vivek, did not respect him – though, outwardly they would act like they loved and respected him. He had become very close to me. He would confide in and discuss with me all his situations – business as well as personal.

As his financial situation was deteriorating day by day, he terminated his senior secretary and other personal staff. The Indian executive and senior government officials have low-educated and low-paid workers for their menial work –

these are called *"peons."* Prem Kumar borrowed my peon, Kadam, who was very sincere, honest, and hardworking. Kadam would keep me updated on Prem Kumar's situation at all times – of course, with his approval. Both Amit and Vivek were gradually taking charge of their father with their mother's support. They first started sharing his grand office, which he did not mind out of love and affection for his children. Initially, he felt happy that finally, his sons were getting serious about the business that he had set up with such hard work. After some time, they suggested to their father that since the factories were closed and there was not much work, he did not need to the office every day and that he could stay at home, resting and meeting his old friends.

He could not sense their sinister plans. Both Amit and Vivek were planning to demolish their father's personal office and make small work cabins, which then could be hired out. Eventually, they started the work of demolishing his office and constructing small work cabins without his consent – though they had their mother's support. Prem Kumar could not do anything. He would never take legal help against his family members. His sons stooped to such a low level that they retained two cabins for themselves and hired out all the remaining work cabins – some even on an hourly basis.

Prem Kumar Gupta did not get even one cabin for his work obligations. Most times, he would have to wait outside until a work cabin became available so that he could carry out his business needs. After that, Amit and Vivek, along with their mother, turned to their gorgeously elegant bungalow at Pedder Road. They sold the bungalow and with that money, bought two penthouses in the newly-carved western suburb of Versova, about 35-40 kilometers away from Pedder Road.

Amit and Vivek took one penthouse each, leaving nothing for their father. He was forced to share accommodation with them. Again, their mother supported them. They did not let him meet any of his friends with whom he could share his plight. He was virtually under house arrest. Due to these extremely stressful situations, he started losing his mental balance.

One day, his wife called me and requested that I see them as Prem Kumar was missing me a lot. I instantly went to see him. While I was there, his wife did not leave him alone with me even for a single moment. She knew how close he was with me and feared that he would tell me about his plight. He was speaking weirdly and incoherently. That was the last time I could see him. No one from his family, not even his wife or two sons for whom I set up their new industrial project with French collaboration, ever contacted me after that. Thus, he was isolated from his friends and well-wishers completely. He was not allowed to see anyone and no one could get in to see him or look after him in any manner possible. This was the tragic end to the story of a man who gave his whole life for the comfort of his wife and children – who did not save anything for himself like most people. He was betrayed in life and was left with no one who truly loved or cared about him.

This is something that I have learned from life – no matter how much you may care about the people around you, they are likely to deceive you once you are not worth anything to them. If it could happen to such great people as Prem Kumar, then who are we to not experience the same in such times of helplessness? I will discuss corruption in more details in the upcoming chapters.

Chapter 10
Indian Corruption Goddess at Her Peak: My Own Projects

It had become my habit of researching new and unique industrial/commercial projects. I had finalized technical joint venture projects with B. F. Goodrich Tires of USA, $100 million joint venture with Isoreg (who delved in power interruption protectors and the Hilton Hotel Group), and other high-profile ventures. During those days, none of my long list of highly resourceful entrepreneurs dared to venture into such large projects from the grass root level.

One medium-sized German entrepreneur, Gebhard Shick, who specialized in high-value flooring materials like marble and granite products and projects, approached me to set up unique marble tiling – a hand labor-oriented project with 100 percent buyback guarantee. Something like this had not been done in India before. It was something different and unique. I decided to undertake this project myself, as I did not feel that anyone else would be able to perform it satisfactorily enough. It involved artistic and skilled manual work. Capital investment was limited. A factory building of 600 square meters with special power-setting regulators on a land of 1,000 square meters to be provided as my contribution and specialized small machinery equipment was to be supplied and installed by the German partner Gebhard Shick of Shick Granit un Marmor. I had to register a separate joint venture company named Indo Deutsche Marmor and Granite Private Limited for this particular project as it could not be completed under a single identity – either my own or theirs.

This project required several licenses for the following.

- Setting up the project.
- Joint venture and technical collaboration.
- Importation of goods.
- Buying foreign currency.
- Exporting, and so on.

The Government of India had introduced several schemes for encouraging export-oriented units, such as Export Free Trade Zones in selective locations throughout India, Santa Cruz Electronics Export Processing Zone in Bombay, and 100% export-oriented units for small and medium industrial units. Under these schemes, all that was required were licenses approved by a single application which was processed and approved by Joint Chief Controller of Imports and Exports (JCCIE). JCCIE would hold monthly meetings on the last Friday of the month to clear all applications submitted by the 21st day of the month. I submitted my application to JCCIE with all the requisite documents in the first week of the month. The staff at JCCIE did not finalize my application and pointed out some shortcomings. I received a letter from them only after the cut-off date of 21st. I submitted the requested documents immediately. Again, I received a letter from the JCCIE after the cut-off date of the 21st of the second month. This continued for more than three months, and still, my application was undergoing the processing system.

This is another classic example of corruption I had to deal with. The problem was, there was simply no one that I could think of who would be able to help me. Since a bribe was never asked directly, I couldn't offer them any kind of bribe to get my application processed quickly enough. As I have mentioned before, I hated this whole attitude and mindset of corruption, but there was little to nothing I could do about it because I had to survive within the system. If there was anything I wanted to get done, it meant that I had to pay a hefty fee for it, no matter how illegal it may be.

This is what I believe is the reason why so many things do not get done in countries like ours and progress becomes generally slow. People are only worried about stuffing their own pockets with money. I, of course, had to face similar problems while trying to establish my business and expanding it. I was attending every monthly meeting. In those days, Rajiv Gandhi had become Prime Minister after the assassination of his mother, Indira Gandhi. He was young blood, and until his assuming the prime minister's role, he would be spending most of his time overseas working as a commercial pilot.

He was married to an Italian lady. Upon becoming Prime Minister, he had several fresh ideas on enhancing the efficiency of the government sector and eliminating corruption. Accordingly, he selected likeminded young ministers. One such minister was Mr. Chidambaram, Industries and Commerce Minister. He was responsible for JCCIE as well.

He addressed one JCCIE monthly meeting when he declared that all applications to JCCIE would be approved within thirty days of submission. In the subsequent monthly meeting, several dissatisfied applicants whose application were pending for over three months, like mine, reminded JCCIE that the minister had promised that all applications would be cleared within thirty days.

To this, the corrupt man promptly said, *"The minister promised, not me."*

My application was not approved for months. I heard that the JCCIE took a large amount (corruption) to expedite the application process, but I had no clue how to approach them. In the meantime, my German partners were so keen to start our project that without even informing me, they shipped the consignment of equipment and product designs, along with samples. It was a legal requirement for Indian Customs that imported goods should not be shipped without the import license on hand. German partners refused to understand the Indian regulations and were insistent on going as per the German system.

My factory was ready with all the fittings, including special power equipment procured locally. The German shipment had arrived and was held by the customs. The JCCIE was taking time, and the customs authorities refused to understand the situation because of the deliberation of the Germans sending their shipment over. Finally, nothing could be done, and this project had to be shelved. My German partners severed all commercial relationships with me as they felt I was not making the right moves and decisions. My first ever project that was all my own died even before its birth. I felt a kind of devastation that I had never felt before. It was like everything I tried my hand at was doomed to failure from the beginning since all the controls were in the hands of corrupt officials. The worst part was that there was nothing I could do about it. I had tried my level best to get the applications cleared, but that had not happened. I had tried explaining the situation to the German clients, but they had failed to understand the inconsistencies in India and blamed me for incompetence. I had worked day and night, yet it was all down the drain simply because a few corrupt people in the system had refused to do what needed to be done in time.

My point here is that many times, the difficulties coming in your life leave you completely helpless because you are not able to sort them out. If there is one thing I have never done is give up. Yes, my heart had gone out because I continued to fail at what I believed could make me into something bigger, but I refused to let these things break me down. I knew that where there was a will, a way would always emerge. I may have lost this deal, but I was sure to find another that would work out much better. So, I decided to let this one go and switch my energy and focus on something else.

After all, life does not end on one failure that one encompasses. My younger brother Anand had been living in Sharjah, UAE since 1977. I used to visit him frequently. In those days, Dubai had started growing at a rapid speed, and construction projects were at their peak. I observed that there was a huge demand for plywood, which was being imported 100% of the time. The Dubai government had set up Jebel Ali Free Trade Zone and was building large industrial buildings with all infrastructure and utilities supplied for leasing out to aspiring entrepreneurs.

I approached them with my project idea of manufacturing plywood. They liked it and instantly granted me a huge industrial building of 10,000 square meters on a long-term lease, with no down payment and one year's payment holiday, meaning the lease payments were to commence after twelve months. I sourced a large plywood manufacturer corporation in India, with whom after negotiation I signed a technical collaboration and procurement of plant and equipment. I then visited large traders of plywood in Dubai and Sharjah, who instantly welcomed my project idea.

They said they had to maintain a large inventory of imported plywood sheets because any import shipment would take 30-45 days from the date of order. They, therefore, had to maintain 45 days stock/inventory. My factory would help them drastically reduce their inventory level. I got unanimous approvals from major traders. After that, I approached the local bank branches of large international banks for the financing of this project. It was quite an attractive project, with guaranteed sales of its products. The banks approved my project for financing, subject to approval from the Government of India.

In those days, there was a restriction on Indian residents to invest abroad. Permission/approval was required from several departments of the government, as well as a clearance from the Reserve Bank of India. This meant I was stuck again. The two main government organizations for granting approvals were Foreign Investment Board, which was headed by the senior most public servant ranked Secretary, and the Reserve Bank of India, headed by a Governor reporting directly to the Prime Minister. These were supposed to be working independently.

Through my senior-level contacts, I knew that I could get access to the Secretary, so I sought an appointment with him. He fixed a dinner meeting for me, along with his family members at an expensive restaurant serving Dum

Pukht style food in a five-star hotel – the Sheraton Tower International in Delhi. I joined him after flying two hours from Bombay. Of course, I booked for five people – me, plus four from his side. Of course, I was to foot the bill. He came with seven people – all family members. The food dishes were priced almost eight times higher than average food prices in a decent, rich ambiance restaurant. Anyway, I was supposed to pay for everyone, whether they were family or officials. He was full of praise for me and my big achievements at such an early age, but did not consider it appropriate to discuss my business application in front of everyone.

The Secretary called me to his office the next working day. When I reached his office, he had called a team of his staff from relevant departments to interview me on my project and its benefits. After discussing my project feasibility, he took a break and took me to the VIP room. He said that it usually took four to six months after all the required documentation was provided.

However, in this case, he could expedite, for which several senior officials had to be satisfied. He quoted an exorbitant amount running into millions to be given to the relevant officials as the bribe. He asked for substantial advance running into millions. This amount was beyond my reach at any point in time. Even though my heart sank upon hearing it, I kept my demeanor calm. I also required approval from the Reserve Bank for remitting funds abroad. He, the Secretary, referred me to his good friend, Deputy Governor of Reserve Bank. Meetings with the Deputy Governor (DG) were cordial and encouraging. The DG showed that he was very pleased with my progress and my new project, and would assist in any way he could. He also spoke aggressively against corruption and vowed that at the Reserve Bank, their system was always clean and the best in the country, helping upcoming entrepreneurs in every way possible.

He strictly warned me against offering any amount to his lower officers, otherwise, he would not progress my application for approval. After five to six meetings throughout three months, he opened his big mouth and demanded 10 million rupees (then equivalent to a US$1 million) down payment to put forward my application. There was no way I could afford that much money. It was not only out of the budget, but it was something I did not even hope to make in years. Combined this with the amount the other official had asked, there was no way I would be able to pay all these corrupt people to simply begin the documentation of the business, let alone the actual business. Here went down my second ambitious project. This disheartened me a lot. As I said before, it seemed like even if I touched gold, it would turn to sand. I started becoming so hopeless that I was unable to keep my optimistic views about life. I had lost interest in my work and started hating the habit of offering bribe money to anyone, even if my clients would pay the corruption money. I became desperate to get out of my consultancy business. It did not seem like the kind of business I would succeed at.

I thought that it would be best for me to do something else for a change. The thing was, I was not sure what it was other than a job or business that I could do. I had tried both, and it was just that corruption was rampant everywhere, without any respite. However, this was not where my troubles ended. On top of everything else that was happening with me on a professional level, I was also facing domestic issues with my wife.

These two projects that I had tried to start had caused severe financial hardships as I had invested a substantial amount in the factory building and equipment for my Indo

Schick Marmor and Granit Private Limited project, as well as in my frequent travel and corruption payments for the Plywood project. This had gotten to my wife, Bhoji, who, under the influence of her childhood friend, Pushpa, had started putting pressure on me to close my Bombay office and work from home, which was 60 kilometers away from Bombay. My wife had failed to understand that my clients, as well as all my influential business friends/clients, would never travel to my home office and that I had no scope of getting any substantial business from my home office. She had become nasty and would mentally torture me every single night. She did not care that every day, after spending 14-15 hours away from home on travel and at work, I would become physically and mentally exhausted. She did not have to travel for work, and we had domestic servants, including a cook, who did all work at home. As such, she did not truly understand the stress I was going through every single day.

My wife knew that I loved both my children to the hilt. She used that as my weakness in her attacks on me. She would frequently threaten me that she would walk out on me, leaving with our two children. Finally, I snapped, unable to take the daily bickering, and sold my beloved office that I had purchased with the generosity of Prem Kumar Khurana. This angered and annoyed him a lot, and permanently damaged our friendship. However, after selling the office, I could not think of moving my work away from the prestigious location of Nariman Point and therefore, I leased a smaller office in the vicinity by paying a substantial deposit. I had modern office equipment, including PCs, newly introduced in India at the time, and a large Xerox machine imported from U.S.A. by Modi Xerox Limited, who were in the process of setting up the first manufacturing unit in India.

At the beginning of my consultancy business, a wealthy businessman, Jay Mehta from my Oriental Bank contacts, approached me. The bank was situated within the huge industrial corporation land of the Official Liquidator – a top-ranked public servant. That industrial area had become a prime real estate property worth hundreds of millions of Indian rupees.

It was commonly known that such properties could be sold to private businesses for development by the Official Liquidator at his sweet whims, and of course, only to the people who were willing to offer huge sums of corruption money. Jay Mehta was a resourceful businessman, but not well educated. He was confident of talking to top government officials. He, therefore, approached me to accompany him to speak to the official liquidator, Ram Paswan.

After extensive research about Ram Paswan, I gathered information on how to approach him directly without involving any middleman. He preferred talking such matters privately – meaning without the submission of any formal application, at his residence, only in the after hours, without prior appointment.

I was advised that we should carry substantial cash with us. His employer, the Government of India, had provided him with a huge apartment in the elite area of Bombay. After giving him prior notice we, I and Jay Mehta, reached his residence. He opened the door himself, wearing casual poor-quality home clothes. He instantly burst out at us, without letting us in, using bad, derogatory terms that started with 'F' words.

Then, suddenly he relaxed and invited us inside. He offered us tea and snacks. His employer, the Indian Government, had provided him domestic servants that served us. Ram Paswan then asked how much cash we had with us. At my advice, Jay Mehta offered him 50,000 rupees. He instantly grabbed the cash and said that it was too little and that in the next meeting, we should give him at least 200,000 rupees. We then carried our talks on the subject matter for an hour. It was like an orientation on the process to commence. He said that we would need numerous meetings with him and called us for the next meeting a week after, reminding us without any hesitation to bring him 200,000 rupees. He said that there were many parties interested in the property that had offered him big cash incentives. Since we were not the only one in the market, he could ask however much he wanted without any fear of losing the customer.

He was not sophisticated in his speech and mannerisms. Rather, he was rough and seemed to come from an uneducated and uncultured family background. The Indian government has a policy of positive discrimination in favor of scheduled castes – people from backward and underprivileged sectors. Under this policy, 20% of all government jobs positions are reserved for these scheduled castes.

Ram Paswan was from this caste, sadly enough. I realized that he must be doing the same with other people as well and gathering money from everyone. I had an extensive discussion with Jay Mehta, explaining to him the process suggested by Ram Paswan. I also expressed my gut feelings that Ram Paswan would not do our work and that he would rather continue calling us for discussions, every time increasing the amount he wanted, without making any settlement. We decided that we would not see him again and instead would submit an official application with supporting documents. However, nothing happened, and we dropped the project idea forever. I did not only lose my money, but also a lot of valuable time as no deed commenced. It appears that my destiny was against me. I accepted my fate quietly as the sweet will of the Almighty. I always remember my mother's childhood words from Guru Nanik, "*Tera bhana mitha lage*" (in Punjabi) addressing the Almighty – meaning, "*Whatever You say is sweet to me.*"

I also remember how later in my life, while traveling for work for Bank of India at Bombay, my friend Kumar used to say, "*Even this will pass away.*" This remains in my memory and continues to haunt me.

In Australia, to my surprise, one day my young son Govinda in his early teens said, *"Everything happens for a reason."* This too still sticks out in my mind.

These sayings give me the strength to face any situation in my life. I continue practicing and professing hope for the best, while simultanously keeping prepared for the worst. My father said to me in my early twenties, *"Power corrupts."* How right he was!

I had seen it with my own eyes. All the officials who had even one iota of power would make sure they abused it for all its worth just for personal gains. People simply could not make life or work easier for others, and if they could, they would cause difficulties so that ease could come their way. Such was the way of the world, and if I wanted to succeed, I would need to have thicker skin and not let anything harsh disappoint me into depression.

Chapter 11
The Letter

As I told you before, I had gotten an invitation letter from the Australian Government inviting me to migrate to Australia with permanent residency (equivalent to Green Card). This invitation letter kept lying in my drawer for over two years without me taking any decision about whether or not I wanted to relocate. I was a huge cricket fan and liked Australia because of its top position in cricket. This may seem like a strange reason for migration, but desperate times call for desperate measures.

Out of my sheer desperation, I responded to the invitation and submitted my application, along with all the requested documents. Call it fate, but within two months, I received approval for the permanent residency – not only for myself, but also for my wife and two children. I had six months to move. Otherwise, the visa would expire on August 10, 1992. For six months, I had been trying to deal with my situation and change the nature of my business. I have mentioned before how broke and depressed I had been, and it was a lot of effort for me to migrate from one country to another – one that was completely unknown to me except for the country's cricket team. Hence, the reason why I kept delaying thinking about it or getting any action involved. I knew that my business deals were not prospering and I would need to decide before it was too late. This was when I decided that I needed to give Australia a chance. So it was in the first week of August 1992 when I started planning to leave for Australia. I prepared my wife and two children and started packing up with minimal items.

I wanted to make sure that it was an entirely new start for us. Hence, I wanted to take as few things as possible. On August 7, which also happened to be my birthday, we departed India for Sydney via Bangkok. We stayed in Bangkok for two days and reached Sydney on August 10, 1992, just hours before the expiration of the visa.

I had decided that closing office would not be a wise move. Therefore, I left it in the hands of a few dedicated employees, and it continued working with three employees – my personal secretary and two clerks. I left my house under the care of my two domestic servants for whom I had constructed a separate living room. As for my factory building, I had already appointed a security guard. My plan was to maintain two residences – one in Bombay and one in Sydney.

This would allow me to travel between Australia and India without much difficulty and also keep a safe plan for me – for if things did not work out in Australia, I could always return to India. My close friend in Bombay requested me to stay with his son, Vicky, who had recently migrated to Sydney with his wife and had a large spare residential place to accommodate my family. He had informed me that his son would come to the airport to pick us up. I, therefore, did not carry any research for residential premises in Sydney, thinking that I could safely leave my family when I returned to Bombay for my office. I had planned to settle my family at this acquaintance's house and return to Bombay in order to continue settling things at my office.

When we arrived at Sydney Airport in the middle of the night, there was no one to receive us. After waiting for half an hour, I called Vicky's home telephone – there were no cell phones then. He told me that his father had misunderstood and that he never had any plans to come to the airport to pick us up. He suggested that we should take a taxi. His house was in the suburb of Maryland, about 50 kilometers away from Sydney CBD. Taking a cab meant we had to spend $60, which was a huge sum of money in Indian currency, but since we were left with no other choice or means of transportation and since it was the dead of the night, we had to do that. Upon arriving at his home, we found to our shock that the huge house his father had claimed his son possessed was a lie. In reality, Vicky was only renting a small apartment that contained two small bedrooms, a lounge, and a small kitchen. We were given one bedroom for the four of us. Not only this, but we were also expected to share the rent along with all the groceries and other expenses, such as utility bills.

Vicky and his wife were extreme misers. They even restricted our use of tissue paper at the dinner table. Though they did not say it in direct words, it was pretty apparent that he had been forced into this situation by his father and did not really want us living with him. Obviously, this could not work. I, therefore, started looking for an alternative independent residence for us, which Vicky and his wife did not like, even though us living with them was a problem for them. I first looked for an apartment close to Sydney CBD. Then, I thought of my family who would be living without me. So I decided to look for a place in a bigger town, close to the railway station and not very far from Vicky's residence.

Parramatta was the town near Merrylands where I decided to settle in a two large bedrooms apartment in a multistory-secured building, in which some Indian families were already living. This apartment was close to the local police station, less than a ten minute walk from Parramatta Railway Station. We moved there within two weeks. During the first month, we traveled a lot like tourists and ended up visiting all the major places of interest.

My children were enjoying, thinking that we were on holiday. My wife was hoping that we would soon move back to India. They had no idea that I was determined to settle in Sydney. This was because I had begun to feel that we had no future in India. Australia might allow us to get bigger and better, not only in terms of finances, but also mentally.

While in Sydney, I explored the feasibility of offering project consultancy services in Australia, and thus started attending business/investment conferences. I set up my company in the name of BMG Watts Corporate Proprietary (Pty) Limited (Ltd) with the help of Price Waterhouse

Coopers (now PWC) using their address as my company's registered office. I met a group of four resourceful businessmen. After getting to know about my professional and consultancy background, they presented their project of extracting gold from gold tailings. Australia is well-known for its rich mineral resources and huge mining industries. The conventional gold mining processes could not extract full gold from the ores and therefore, large volumes of earth waste, called tailings, were thrown out. It cost huge money to clear the sites of such waste. These four businessmen had come together and acquired a newly developed magnetic extraction technology's rights. They were looking for more partners to finance the project. The required equipment was highly pricy, and the project needed large industrial premises. I had several meetings with them at different locations in Sydney, Melbourne, and Brisbane.

None of my Indian business contacts would invest in an overseas project, that too a greenfield untested project. My Australian connections were not mature, and I soon realized that they would not dare to put their funds in a large unknown industrial project. This meant that I again faced the same brick wall I had been facing in India. The project did not progress further because people were unwilling to take the risk. Thereafter, another group of businessmen approached me with regard to a holiday resort project in Vanuatu, a well-known holiday destination, which had not been explored much then.

It was a good project, but none of my contacts was willing to invest in it either. I was beginning to wonder if I would ever be able to hit it big with my consultancy business. It seemed that no matter what I tried my hand at or where, things would not go as I wanted them to and even though talks were held, this was the only road I would be able to walk. There simply was no fruition to the projects I came across.

I soon realized that Australia's business scenario was completely different. High labor cost, high property cost along with rentals, an absence of government-owned land corporations like MIDC in India, and an absence of banking support for small and medium-sized businesses the way it was in India, were some of the major stumbling blocks.

I then took admission at the University of Technology Sydney to obtain a Masters' degree in Project Management.

However, soon I came to understand that there was no use of this degree for me in continuing my business. Therefore, I dropped it. I decided to pursue Accounting and Taxation practice, for which certification for public practice was needed from an accounting body, like the Australian Institute of Chartered Accountants or Australian Association of Certified Practicing Accountants (CPA), which later changed its name to CPA Australia. For this, I was first required to study advanced level Australia Taxation Law, Australian Corporation Law, and Australian Accounting Reporting Standards. For this, I had to study four subjects, for thirteen weeks, two days a week. I did all papers in three months from two universities, with a high distinction – the University of Sydney and the University of Technology Sydney.

Thereafter, I was required to study five more papers, each with annual study for the CPA program, which I completed in one year. These are some of my achievements I am truly proud of as they required hard work and utmost dedication, and I was able to handle them in remarkable time. I had planned to stay alternatively for one month in Sydney and one month in Bombay until I finalized my plans for whether or not I wanted to maintain my Bombay office.

This continued for eighteen months, during which period I shuttled nine times between Sydney and Bombay. During those days, any emigrant in the PR (permanent resident) category was entitled to register immediately upon arrival for the social security benefits with Centrelink – the Australian government agency responsible for the management of the social security benefits scheme. I registered the whole family of four the very next day. According to it, my family would get financial support for unemployment until my wife or I found suitable employment. This gave me peace of mind as my family would get financial support in my absence. Within a year, my wife got a part-time job in a public hospital. We were off the social security benefits and never looked back – never again finding the need to use social security benefits. This took some time, but the happiness it granted us was immense. I still look back at that one year and wonder how far we have come from our humble times.

It appeared that India was not willing to take me back. One day, while I was in Sydney, my personal secretary called me from Bombay and informed me that the landlord, Ashok Thappar, had forcibly snatched office keys from her and kicked my staff out. I rushed back to Bombay, but could not take my office back. The landlord had locked the office and gone back to his base in Delhi. He refused to budge, saying it was his property and he could do whatever he wanted with it. He refused to come to Bombay or indulge in any dialog or negotiation. Through my contacts, I approached the Assistant Police Commissioner (ACP), who soon became friends with me.

He successfully managed to get me my equipment, furniture, and records back. Ashok Thappar had also appropriated my large deposit amount. For the office premises, I had to go to the High Court, which was not practical. The matter would be in the court forever, and the legal fees would be exorbitant. This was something I did not want to get involved in, knowing that it would be completely futile to waste the money. I would still probably not be able to get the justice I so desperately needed. Hence, I decided not to go down that road.

I also knew that no matter how good you are with officials, you still need to bribe them to get any of your work done. So, I continued giving gifts to the ACP, but it seemed that he wasn't satisfied and asked me to gift him a Rado Swiss Watch on my subsequent visits to Bombay. I purchased a Rado watch for $1,200 and presented it to him. He started laughing and said that it was a *"ladies"* watch. He asked for a heavy-duty watch, which was worth more than $10,000. This was something I had neither time and nor money for, so I gave him cash and kept the watch with me. I still have it. Thus, my Bombay office was gone, and I returned to Sydney empty-handed and defeated. I remember the look of disdain my wife gave me without uttering a single word upon my return on a morning when she was getting ready for her work. It cut me from deep within, but there was no retort that I could give her. I know she thought that I was an utter failure, but only I knew how hard I had worked and how much I had tried to change things. The only thing I can say is that it was fate that was constantly dealing me a hard hand.

I had appointed a security guard at my Ambernath factory building. Earlier, I had helped set up a paper packaging, box manufacturing unit, close to factory, for my wife's childhood friend Pushpa's husband and brother. Pushpa started suggesting to Bhoji that there was no need to spend so much money on the security guard when they (Pushpa and her family) could keep the surveillance.

One day, they removed the security guard without my

knowledge. Soon thereafter, the person from whom I had purchased the factory building entered the building and took possession, claiming that he was still the owner. I was already frustrated with the loss of my office and had no desire to fight anyone anymore. No one, not even Pushpa's husband, Bhoji's brothers, or my brothers-in-law were willing to have any dialog with Narang or represent me in any legal action.

Thus, my factory was also gone. I was lost about how to reclaim it since I was sitting so far away and there didn't seem to be anyone back in India who was willing to take up the fight for me. So I let it all go without making any efforts. During this period, while I was in grief, my wife Bhoji started giving me extreme terrors about my family. I could understand her plight. She, by now, was convinced that we would not go back to Bombay, and it affected her psyche badly. Both my children were getting used to their life in Sydney, but she was not happy about it because she could see the children and I settling in, unlike her.

One day, while I still had my Bombay office, she said to me that she would give air bubble injection to my children when they were asleep, and they would not wake up the next day. This frightened me immensely and hastened my plans to permanently stay in Sydney with my family. She wanted us to go back, but I was determined to stay right in Sydney and make our lives there.

Thereafter, I decided never to visit Bombay and sell my house. In India, even today, anyone can enter an empty property and claim it as his own. They can generate authentic-looking property documents in their name, backdated by 25 years. My house in Ulhasnagar was huge, like a palace, which I had built passionately over the years using the money I had made from the consultancy business. I had to sell that house in distress for a meager 1.4 million rupees (then equivalent to $60,000). Had I not and still gone to Sydney, it is highly likely some stranger would have squatted there and claimed it as their own. I brought that amount to Sydney and thus, all my properties were gone. It was most definitely not the way I had wished for things to end, but I could see no other choice. Therefore, I accepted the losses and decided to move on with what I had been able to procure.

I did not go back to Bombay to meet any of my relatives or friends for over eight years. This saddened me greatly, but I could not risk the lives of my children while they were alone with my wife. In 1995, I purchased a house in a highly regarded residential area of Castle Hill. This house was on a land block of 1,000 square meters and had eleven rooms altogether. This was like our dream home, and my first office in Sydney was home. My children were very happy to have a big house once again, similar to the one we had in Bombay. For three years in Australia, they had become quite distressed thinking that we had become poor and could not afford a bigger house.

But thankfully, I was able to return to them the lifestyle they were used to. In the absence of local experience, I could not start my accounting practice immediately. Hence, I decided to look for a job. Unfortunately, I found it hard as I had no local experience. Through my wife's work contact, Jean Ireland, I managed to get unpaid work as an assistant to an accounts section in a large Sothern Cross Retirement Village where Jean's husband John was the managing director.

Within three months, I landed a part-time paid job as a finance officer in the New South Wales Institute of Psychiatry, affiliated with the NSW Health Department. This was the time when our life started changing. This was also the place where I got to know that no matter how hard I may try to run from corruption, it would not leave me alone and in peace.

I will explore more details of my experiences in Australia in the next few chapters where you will discover just how corruption infiltrated our societies – be it in the east or west. I have learned in my life that it is inescapable and no matter how much you may make the effort of not getting involved in this filthy business, it refuses to let you remain clean and pure. It is a sad reality that I have accepted and am hoping that by reading my experiences, it will make things easier for your conscience, because there really is no out.

Chapter 12
A New Beginning – Australia

There is a reason why people decide to migrate from one place to the other. They want a better source of income, they want something more for their families and themselves than just the kind of living they have, or they are trying to escape something. For me, it was all three things, but the last one more than anything else. I was sick and tired of the corruption and deceit that I had to face in India when it came to officials and to professional life.

It was basically the corruption in India that forced me to move away. I was eager to continue my career in a world free from corruption and people who only knew how to use one another. But alas, such was not to be my fate! When we had first landed in Australia, we were very pleased with the efficiency of the government offices in Sydney. Registration with the Australian Taxation Office was the first step we were required to complete before any other registration process. We entered the Taxation Office and received excellent service and guidance. Our registration was done instantly without any kind of hassle or bribery. We then visited the Centrelink Office for registration for social security and unemployment benefits, then Medicare registration for all four of us, and interim cards for instant use. All other required registrations and bank account acquisition went more smoothly than we could ever have dreamed of.

This was unimaginable in India. Even today after tremendous progress and advanced automation in India, it would be hard to find such efficiency in the government offices of India. My children, Moksha and Govinda, got settled in their schools. My wife Bhoji got a full-time job in a government hospital. She went ahead to study and complete her post-graduate degree in Master of Clinical Chemistry from Western Sydney University. All of this was done literally without a hitch.

I too settled in better than I could hope for. I got a part-time job, initially two days a week, at the New South Wales Institute of Psychiatry, which was quite interesting. What amazed me was the fact that the accounting staff did not have much experience in professional accounting. The senior-most person in the accounting department, Gus, a Chinese guy, who had been working there for over ten years, was neither intelligent nor knowledgeable. He was arrogant and behaved as if he was the supreme hero who knew everything and more. All the accounts were maintained manually, and the preparation of any significant reporting document was an absolute nightmare. The staff had just the basic skills in Microsoft Excel. Since the institute was a top-class academic body in that particular state, the volume of transactions was massive and seemingly unending.

I was the only qualified accounting professional in the entire company, which was why I was asked to take charge of the accounting section. Gus, it was pretty apparent, did not like this and refused to cooperate with me on anything. He felt that his authority was being undermined since the work was given to a newcomer, who was not only new to work, but was also new to the country. I decided to leave him be and do the best I could for the accounts department of the company.

I suggested that a proper accounting software should be implemented urgently, as that would unburden the work of the people involved and give more accurate results. The management instantly approved my idea and authorized me to purchase and install a suitable accounting software. I acquired the Attaché 5 accounting software and trained myself first, and then the accounting staff of three, including Gus and two ladies. During the period of installation and training, I worked full time for five days. After three months, I reverted to part time activities, three days a week. I became the Chief Financial Officer of the institute, and soon my position was made full time. Director Dr. Tony Williams headed the institute, who was in his late fifties at that time.

He was drawing a handsome salary along with many perks. He was assisted by the deputy director (part time) Ms. Jenny and manager Robert Fritchley. There was no internet banking then, and all deposits and payments were made manually. The joint signatories to the checks were Tony Williams, Jenny, and Robert. This meant that the signature of any two of these three people would be valid for affirmation. Even though I was Chief Finance Officer, Tony Williams, and Robert refused to add me as a signatory.

Robert would rarely be absent from the office. This resulted in him accumulating a large number of leaves, much above the allowed limit. This was the reason why he was forced to take his designated leaves. Otherwise, the excess accumulated leaves would have expired. Even when he was on leaves, he would constantly be in touch with the office through his confidante assistant, a Lebanese lady, and would frequently visit the office. Of course, all of this was done with Tony's knowledge. In his absence, I would be acting as manager, but he advised the staff not to act on my instructions on any administrative matters without his confirmation. This alerted my *corruption* sense, like a déjà vu of Bank of India, Ulhasnagar branch. I could not help but make the connections of human nature, no matter what part of the world they belonged to.

Tony was a strange man, a perpetual patient of what we call Mondayitis. He would often fall sick on Mondays. For urgent matters, Robert would go to his home for instructions. Robert had been working there for over 25 years as a manager and never sought any promotion, as he did not wish to go away from his office at North Parramatta. This was something that I found extremely strange. Why in the world would any person not seek a promotion or forward motion in their career?

I soon found that there was a secret professional relationship between Tony and Robert. Jenny, on the other hand, a third of the authority in the institute, was a good, honest, and knowledgeable person. He would not dare to go against the wish of the director, Tony. Robert would sign the bank checks, and in the absence of Tony, Jenny would blindly countersign as the second signatory. Tony was required to be out of the institute most days as he had to attend conferences. He would have to go for training sessions and visiting different hospitals, as well as government departments. He would also have to look after some consultancy assignments. Over the years, he had built a very good rapport with seniors at the State Health Department and similar psychiatry institutions all over Australia and neighboring smaller countries, like Papua New Guinea, Samoa Islands, Fiji, and New Zealand. The institute was regularly tendering assignments to provide teaching packages, running workshops, and consultancy by these countries.

The process of tendering was quite elaborate. It required summaries and detailed descriptions of the contents of deliverables along with costing budget. While Tony and Jenny were expert in the technical aspects, they would struggle with the costing aspects of it all. Every time they were required to measure costs, they would start working on costing formula from scratch, and each person would use their own method of raw calculation. They would not care if the institute was even able to recover all the relevant costs. Initially, they would not ask for my assistance thinking that it was their area of expertise. One day, when the manager was budgeting the costs, he approached me to ask if I could guide him with some of the sections. I took the whole document and started working on the cost estimates. I designed an Excel spreadsheet and calculated the cost of each element that would remain unchanged for each project. When they would later work on it, they would just need to put in the variables for each project.

It allowed me a sort of 'in' with the whole thing, just as I wanted to. I knew things could be vastly improved if they were computerized, but since no one was willing to ask for help, I could not offer it myself as they would have felt threatened with my intrusion. Over time, I standardized the costing form for them, with fixed cost items and rates already incorporated.

All they had to do was put in information on the quantum specific to the project for which they had designed the contents and number of hours/days required to complete the project. Soon, the director, Tony Williams, realized that the institute was going broke with each project. However, he had no remorse and was convinced that he was doing a great public service for the people from backward countries. He was the only person delivering service – for which the institute was awarded a contract due to its competitive bids. His salary was substantial, nearly three times of the similarly qualified people capable of delivering the service. On top of all this were the perks that he was receiving – first-class travel, five-star accommodation, etc. It was something that most other people in his position could not even dream of. Tony Williams was under the previous senior government employees, who enjoyed generous superannuation/provident scheme under which the government would match the employee's personal contributions.

He was contributing one-third of his salary toward superannuation and his employer, the government, contributed a similar amount. This direct cash government contribution was available to a select group of government employees, and no one else at the institute had this benefit. The income tax rate on superannuation contribution and income on the investment was highly subsidized.

All this made his daily charge rate quite high – four times that of the next professional capable of delivering consultancy assignments. One column of the standard project cost sheet that I prepared for the institute included a charge rate for each person involved in the project, starting from content writing. It was most often handled by Jenny and another technical staff, Nicola. He was designated to deliver the project, primarily holding workshops, travel, accommodation, incidental costs, and other related items that were common to most projects. Another column that was required in the sheets was the quantum/quantity of each charge item. This was estimated during the writing of the content and would vary for each project. Another column was for the total cost, which had a set formula multiplying the charge rate with the quantity. I included suitable rows and columns for the insertion of the variable information typical to each project. This would generate the total cost of the project in question.

We, with the approval from Tony Williams, had agreed on the charge rates for various activities and personnel. As Tony's charge was coming out high, he asked it to be discounted by 25 percentage points. Jenny, Robert, and Nicola found my standardized cost sheet very handy, useful, and time-saving. They started using it for preparing cost analysis for bidding, project tenders, and more. Initially, they asked me to verify their calculations before submitting them for the competitive tender process. This worked well, and they were pleased that they were able to generate revenue for the institute after recovering all costs. For bigger projects that would be delivered by Tony Williams, the costing looked enormous to him, and he would say that with these projects' costing budget for the institute would be outpriced by the competitors. As such, they would then depute a junior person for project delivery. As these were Tony's favorite projects, so much so that he wanted to deliver them himself every time, he was keen to get the projects at any cost. He was least bothered about whether the institute, which was wholly owned by the government, would incur a loss on the project.

He would ask me point-blank if I could not play with the costing estimates, which were based on actual figures. Of course, changing charge rates was done at his discretion. Unsurprisingly, he started using discretion liberally and frequently. I could not believe what I was seeing. Did the same corruption take place in a country like Australia, with so many of rules, laws, and regulations? How was it possible that this corrupt man did not give a care about the institute that he was working for and was only interested in cheating the authorities for his own gains? My mind was boggled with this fact that something so serious could happen in an advanced country.

I subsequently learned that he was planning for his early retirement and building his database for individual consultancy services post-retirement. Hence, my suspicion of corrupt practices began. Déjà vu, India! I could not imagine that I would again be in the world of corruption, and that too far away from India.

I will give more details about the kind of corruption and diplomacy I had to face in Australia in the upcoming chapters. It will give you an idea that no matter what civilized nation you are a part of, corruption is something that is truly not escapable.

Chapter 13
The Australian Corruption

I wish I had known everything about corruption, but it was still not done with me. Everything I hoped I had escaped in India found me once again in a new country. Here, we will discuss the kind of corruption I experienced in Australia. Australia is no doubt a developed country – a member of the G20 developed countries. Western civilization in Australia is a relatively new one. It is thus appropriate to understand the history of so-called civilized Australia.

History of Australia

Australia Day is the official national day of Australia. Celebrated annually on 26th of January, it marks the anniversary of the 1788 arrival of the First Fleet of British ships at Port Jackson, New South Wales, and the rise of the Flag of Great Britain at Sydney Cove by Governor Arthur Phillip. However, to many Aboriginal and Torres Strait Islander people, it represents the beginning of the loss of their land, people, and culture. For them, it was the Invasion Day.

To many, Australia Day symbolizes the beginning of the mourning still felt by indigenous people. That mourning includes intergenerational trauma, along with the loss of sovereign land rights, the loss of family, and the loss of the right to practice their culture and language. It will always be a day of survival, too. Despite colonization, Aboriginal and Torres Strait Islander people survived. Their culture continues to survive. Conversely, the *civilized* Australians are proud of their Convict history.

Who Were the Convicts?

The late 18th century was a period of immense social and political change. France was reeling from revolution and America had just gained independence. In Britain, the industrial revolution had driven thousands of poverty-stricken country folks to the cities. As a new underclass dependent on crime emerged, the prisons were overflowing, and the hangman had his work cut out dealing with the perpetrators of serious offenses. In 1787, the establishment urgently needed a solution to the problem of the burgeoning prison population. The botanist from Captain Cook's discovery hit upon the idea of Botany Bay, Australia. It was not the ideal choice because the place had only been seen once and the 15,000-mile voyage would take more than eight months to complete. Nevertheless, between 1788 and 1868, 165,000 British and Irish convicts made the arduous journey to an unknown land that we now call Australia. The majority of the 165,000 convicts transported to Australia were poor and illiterate, victims of the poor laws and social conditions in Georgian England. Eight out of ten prisoners were convicted of larceny of some variety or another, and transported to the unknown land.

Apart from unskilled and semi-skilled laborers from Britain and Ireland, those transported came from astonishingly varied ethnic backgrounds: American, Corsican, French, Hong Kong, Chinese, West Indian, Indian, and African. There were political prisoners and the prisoners of war, as well as a motley collection of professionals, such as lawyers, surgeons, and teachers.

The average age of the people transported was 26, and their numbers also included children who were either convicted of crimes or were making the journey with their mothers. Just one in six of the transported was a woman. Depending on the offense, the first forty years of transportation convicts were sentenced to terms of seven years, ten years, or life.

Transportation

Prisoners condemned to transportation knew there was little chance they would see their homeland or their loved ones again. Even if they survived the long, cruel journey, they did not know what fate awaited them in a land on the other side of the world.

Relatively few convicts returned home, partly because the system of reprieves extended to only a few and partly because they tended to settle in Australia. Three-quarters of the convicts were unmarried when they left home, so those who found a partner during the voyage or once they arrived in Australia were not likely to leave them behind.

Nevertheless, transportation was a terrifying prospect. Detained prisoners awaited their fate by spending their days and nights in the rotting hulks of old warships transformed into makeshift prisons, rammed up against the mud at Portsmouth Harbour and London's Royal Docklands.

Hulks and Love Tokens

Holed up in the hulks and awaiting the dreaded voyage to begin, it was a common practice for the transported people to spend their days engraving love tokens that they would give our as final mementos to friends and family. Many used the 1797 copper cartwheel penny and the inscriptions range from just the name and date of deportation to elaborate poems and etchings of convicts in chains and boats. Professional engravers were even allowed on board the hulks where prisoners would commission them to craft a poignant keepsake on their behalf.

The Voyage

The journey was long and hard. For the first twenty years, prisoners were chained up for the entire eight months at sea. The cells were divided into compartments by wooden or iron bars. On some ships, as many as 50 convicts used to be crammed into one compartment.

Discipline was brutal, and the officers themselves were often illiterate, drunk, and cruel. They recruited their crews from waterside taverns. They were hardened thugs who would not shrink from imposing the toughest punishment on a convict who broke the rules.

Disease, scurvy, and seasickness were rife. Although only 39 of the 759 convicts on the first fleet died, conditions deteriorated. By the year 1800, one in 10 prisoners died during the voyage. Many convicts lost up to ten teeth due to scurvy, and outbreaks of dysentery made conditions foul in the suffocating, confined space below deck. Convict ships transporting women inevitably became floating brothels, where women were subjected to varying degrees of degradation. In fact, in 1817, a British judge acknowledged that the younger women were to be taken to the cabins of the officers each night or thrown in with the crew.

For those convicts who disembarked in Sydney Cove in 1788, however, the first Australia Day was a bewildering experience. Unused to their land legs, they stumbled, cursing through the uncultivated wood where they had landed. It was two weeks before enough tents and huts were constructed for the female convicts to disembark. Amid a gale, they held the first bush party in Australia – dancing, singing, and drinking while the storm raged and couples wedged themselves between the red, slimy rocks.

The Aborigines

The aboriginal people lived in Australia, undisturbed by white men, for sixty thousand years before the arrival of the first fleet. For them, the arrival of the convicts was catastrophic. Their first encounter with their new neighbors was the site of a huge orgy on the beach. At first, the Aborigines pitied the prisoners and could not understand the cruelty of the soldiers toward them. Gradually, the convicts began to resent the rations and clothing the Aborigines received and took to stealing their tools and weapons to sell to the sailors as souvenirs. In May 1788, a convict was found speared in the bush, and a week later, two more were murdered.

In the ensuing clashes, between 2,000 and 2,500 Europeans and more than 20,000 Aborigines were killed. The convicts felt the need to establish a class below themselves. Australian racism toward the Aboriginal people originated from the convicts and gradually percolated up through society. This marked the beginning of a bitter, painful battle for the survival of Aboriginal culture, which has raged for more than 200 years up to this day.

Convict Life

A convict's life was neither easy, nor pleasant. The work was hard, accommodation rough and ready, and the food not too palatable. Nevertheless, the sense of community offered small comforts when convicts met up with their mates from the hulks back home or with others transported on the same ship.

Convict Work

Male convicts were brought ashore a day or so after their convoy landed. They were marched up to the Government Lumber Yard, where they were stripped, washed, and inspected, after which they had their vital statistics recorded.

If convicts were skilled, such as carpenters, blacksmiths, or stonemasons, they may have been retained and employed in the government program. Otherwise, they were assigned to labor work or given over to property owners, merchant, or farmers – people who may have once been convicts themselves.

Convict Diet

A convict's daily ration was by no means substantial. Typically, it consisted of:

Breakfast: A roll and a bowl of skilly (a porridge-like dish made from oatmeal), water, and, if they were lucky, meat scraps.

Lunch: It was a large bread roll and a pound of dried, salted meat.

Dinner: It was one bread roll and if they were lucky, a cup of tea.

As if this was not enough to turn your stomach, the officials had an unpleasant cure for hangovers and drunkenness, which they imposed on convicts who were overly fond of rum. The 'patient' was forced to drink a quart of warm water containing a wineglass full of spirits and five grains of tartar emetic. He was then carried to a darkened room, in the center of which was a large drum onto which he was fastened. The drum was revolved rapidly, which made the patient violently sick. He was then put to bed, supposedly disgusted by the smell of spirits.

Convict Clothing

Until 1810, convicts were permitted to wear ordinary civilian clothes in Australia. The new Governor, Lachlan Macquarie, wanted to set the convicts apart from the increasing number of free settlers who were flocking to Australia. The distinctive new uniform marked out the convicts very clearly. The pants had the letters PB, for Prison Barracks, marked on them. The trousers were also buttoned down the sides of the legs, which meant they could be easily removed over a pair of leg irons.

Convict Class System

A class system evolved amidst the convict community. The native-born children of convict couples were known as 'currency,' whereas the children of officials were known as 'sterling.'

A wealthy class of 'Emancipists' (former convicts) sprung up when the governor began to integrate reformed convicts to the fledgling society. These Emancipists, who often employed convicts in their turn, were very much despised by the soldiers and free-exclusives that had come to Australia of their own volition.

Convict Housing

For those convicts who remained in Sydney, lodgings were made available in a neighborhood called *The Rocks*. It was a relatively free community, with few restrictions on daily life. Here, husbands and wives were assigned to each other, and even convicts who were still under sentence opened some businesses. The Rocks became notorious for their drunkenness, prostitution, filth, and thieving. In 1819, Governor Macquarie built Hyde Park Barracks, which afforded greater security. Their employers often gave those sent to work in other towns or the bush food and lodging. The road projects and penal colonies offered far less comfortable accommodations, often with 20 sweaty bodies crammed into a small hut.

Tattoos

When convicts arrived in Australia, detailed reports were compiled of their physical appearance, including distinguishing marks. At the beginning of the 19th century, one in four convicts was tattooed. Although, it was hard to understand what these may have meant to the individual fully – some were interesting, even witty comments on convict's life.

Some tattoos appeared to be poignant love tokens and permanent reminders of the life and loved ones they left behind. Others were cheeky remonstrations with the officials, such as the words *'Strike me fair, stand firm, and do your duty.'*

Similarly, a crucifix tattooed on a convict's back would give the impression that Christ himself was being flogged and angels were standing by with a cup to catch the blood. This implies that it is the authorities that are sinful.

Convict Women

Women made up 15% of the convict population. They were reported to be low-class women, foul-mouthed, and having loose morals. Nevertheless, they were told to dress in clothes from London. With this done, they were lined up for inspection so that the officers could take their pick of the prettiest.

Until they were assigned work, women were taken to the 'Female Factories,' where they performed menial tasks like making clothes or toiling over washtubs. It was also the place where women were sent as a punishment for misbehaving if they became pregnant or had illegitimate children.

Other punishments for women included an iron collar fastened around the neck or having their head shaved as a mark of disgrace. Often, these punishments were for moral misdemeanors, such as being *'found in the yard of an inn in an indecent posture for an immoral purpose,'* or *'misconduct in a brothel.'*

As women were a scarcity in the colony, if they married, they could be assigned to free settlers. Often, desperate men would go looking for a wife at the Female Factories.

Pardon and Punishment

Tickets of leave were granted after four years for those with a seven-year sentence, six years for a fourteen-year sentence, and eight-years for life. The principal superintendent looked at the applications and depending on how much extra punishment the prisoner had received, he would decide to recommend the ticket or not.

A ticket of leave would exempt convicts from public labor and allow them to work for themselves. After this, a prisoner might receive a conditional pardon, which meant he was free but had to stay in Australia, or absolute pardon, which meant he was free to return to England.

If a prisoner was uncooperative or committed further crimes, there was an equally well-defined scale of punishment he would receive: first, working on a road gang, then being sent to a penal colony, and finally capital punishment. There were also a number of incidental punishments a prisoner could receive, such as flogging, solitary confinement, treadmill, the stocks, food deprivation, and thumbscrews.

Flogging

A prisoner was sentenced to flogging by a magistrate. There would be a scourger present, a surgeon, and a drummer to count the beats. Often, floggings were carried out in public, as a warning to other convicts to not commit the same offense. Indeed, there are Australians alive today who remember the horrific scars borne by their grandparents as a result of brutal floggings.

On Norfolk Island, an instrument called a cat'o nine tails was used to flog the convicts. This was a whip made of leather strands, with a piece of lead attached to each thong. The lead would tear deep into the flesh with each stroke, and the only effective relief from the agony it inflicted was to urinate on the ground and then lie down with the open wounds on it.

Australian Penal Colonies

The conditions in the penal colonies were exceptionally harsh. Prisoners who re-offended were sent to the colonies, and it was unlikely they would ever be freed under the system of reprieves.

Macquarie Harbor Penal Station

The natural prison built in the middle of Macquarie Harbor, known as Sarah Island, was meant to be escape-proof. It was surrounded by an impenetrable rainforest, and very few escape attempts were recorded. The convicts who were sent to Sarah Island were often escapees from other penal colonies. Others were skilled men whose task was to build ships.

The convicts were required to cut down the massive Huen Pines, lash the logs together, and raft them down the river. They would work twelve hours a day in cold water, in leg-irons under the continual scrutiny of the guards. Not surprisingly, their main objective was to escape.

Norfolk Island

Fifteen hundred miles off the coast of New South Wales

was the most brutal prison of the convict period. Its name was Norfolk Island. The British wanted an institution that would act as a deterrent in the colony – one so bad that it would terrify even those in Britain who heard its name.

Sir Thomas Brisbane once wrote, *'I wish it to be understood that the felon who is sent there is forever excluded from all hope of return.'* Indeed, a high number of prisoners preferred suicide to enduring the abominable conditions there. Others poisoned burned or blinded themselves in attempts to avoid work. Their physical and mental health suffered due to interminable hard labor, poor diet, overcrowding, coarse, uncomfortable clothing, and harsh punishments such as flogging with cat'o nine tails, and chained to the floor.

The men lived forever in the shadow of the 'Murderers Mound,' where 12 of the convicts who participated in an uprising in July 1846 were executed. Tales from Norfolk Island filtered back to England, and the colony was eventually abandoned in 1855.

Port Arthur

After the closure of Norfolk Island, offenders were sent to the southern tip of Tasmania to a colony called Port

Arthur. Prison reformers back in Britain wanted to experiment with new forms of punishment. The centerpiece of the new institution was the Model Prison. The idea was to replace flogging and corporal punishment with complete sensory deprivation, which would break their spirit and turn them into good citizens.

The guards wore slippers, and carpets in the hallways deadened all sounds. When the convicts were allowed out of their cells, they were made to wear masks so they could not recognize one another. There was very little verbal communication.

Regardless, if you are going to escape from prison, Australia is hardly the easiest place to hitch a ride home to achieve that end. Nonetheless, here were some incredible tales of the few who made a break for it.

John Donahue and the Bushrangers

Bushrangers are seen as heroes in Australia, representing rebellion and triumph over authority. The most celebrated bushranger of them all was John Donahue, a young Dubliner who was sentenced to transportation for life in 1823.

After his escape, John roamed the bush, besieging the settlers and living off a life of plunger. He used to hang out in the caves near Picton. He was eventually shot dead in 1830 by a policeman, and his tale is immortalized in the Ballad of Bold Jack, which was banned at the time as a treason song.

Sarah Island

The penal colony at Sarah Island was meant to have been impossible to escape from. More than 180 escape attempts are known to have been made, but only a few were successful. Most escapees perished in the rainforest and many returned voluntarily after a few days. Some did make it, though. Alexander Pearce escaped Sarah Island twice and survived by eating his companions. He later told his companions that he preferred human flesh to normal food.

Another great tale is of the convicts who stole Cyprus, which was a supply vessel carrying a group of convicts to Macquarie Harbor. They seized the vessel on its route, dumped the officers and crew off board, and sailed off to Japan where they pretended to be shipwrecked British mariners. They were all sent back to Britain as poor starving shipwrecked sailors. Unfortunately, one of them was strolling through London town where he met the ex-police constable from Hobart town, who happened to recognize his tattoos.

William Buckley

William Buckley escaped from Sorrento in Victoria in 1803. He spent 30 years living with the Aborigines and wore a long beard and kangaroo skins. When he returned to civilization, he had completely forgotten the English language and had to learn to speak again. He was completely pardoned and eventually became a respected civil servant.

Convicts and the Colonization of Australia, 1788-1868

The white European's colonization of Australia provides a very revealing chapter in Britain's empire building history. Uncharacteristically for a British punishment, penal transportation involved mass exile, coerced labor, invasion, dispossession, and genocide. This combination of convict stain and colonization was so inglorious that for decades, the history was not written. Instead, Australia was characterized as born by the gold rush, and a working man's paradise ensued out of a vacuum – as if by magic. More recently, the 'History Wars' exposed a huge unease within Australia about how to think of its penal past. A focus on negative aspects was denigrated as the 'black armband' view of the nation's history, inviting the retort of 'white blindfold' for those accentuating the positive.

Convict Colonics

There were two major convict colonies: New South Wales (1788-1840) and Van Diemen's Land (later Tasmania, 1803-1853). Swan River (Western Australia) became a third penal colony when the failing settlement requested an injection of convict laborers (1850-1868). The country of origin, colonial distribution, and gender breakdown of convicts is given in the adjacent figure.

The premier site in convict Australia was Sydney, NSW. The First Fleet sailed into Botany Bay on the 18th of January, 1788, but they quickly assessed conditions as unsuitable and shifted north to Port Jackson (Sydney Harbour) on the 26th January, now marked as Australia Day/Invasion Day, depending upon the perspective. A satellite colony was also established over 1,000 miles away at Norfolk Island, both for strategic imperial reasons and as a food basket in an attempt to overcome incipient famine in the early years at Sydney Cove.

In Van Diemen's Land, a second major convict colony followed at Sullivans Cove (Hobart) with a further outpost at Patersonia (Launceston) in the north of the island. An initial complement of convicts was sent in 1804, but convicts did not start to arrive regularly in Hobart until 1818, by which time the colony had its own Lieutenant Governor (from 1813 onwards).

Origins and Destinations of Australia's Convicts

Other smaller convict establishments developed across the continent. NSW then stretched along the eastern coast of Australia, encompassing territories that would later become the modern-day states of Queensland and Victoria.

Smaller convict establishments were developed at Moreton Bay (now Brisbane) and Port Phillip (now Melbourne) effectively from 1835.

While the latter is sometimes seen as 'convict-free,' it received convicts via Sydney and directly received convict 'Exiles' during 1846-50. This was an experiment whereby a convict who had completed part of their sentence in a British prison was granted a Conditional Pardon or Ticket-of-Leave, and then sent to the colony.

Moreton Bay functioned as a place of 'secondary punishment.' Colonial reoffending could be punished with transportation, and several dedicated penal settlements were dotted around the colonies. They came to include Norfolk Island (resettled for this purpose in 1825), Newcastle (1804), Port Macquarie (1821), Macquarie Harbor (1822), and Maria Island (1825, later a Probation Station). The latter two were replaced by the iconic Port Arthur on the Tasman Peninsula (1830).

There were many experiments and penal innovations made in the Australian convict colonies. Of particular note is the Point Puer establishment at Port Arthur for the reformation of criminal boys, marking a fundamental shift in the conceptualization of juvenile offenders and in the rehabilitation of criminals.

South Australia (1834) received no convicts directly. However, there was a Newgate connection as the colony's development that was shaped by the 'art of colonization' enunciated by Edward Gibbon Wakefield, who was a politician, as well as scoundrel imprisoned for the Shrigley abduction. The territories (Northern and Australian Capital) gained independent existences much later. Australia became an independent nation on 1st January, 1901, when the British Parliament passed legislation allowing the six Australian colonies to govern in their own right as part of the Commonwealth of Australia. The Commonwealth of Australia was established as a constitutional monarchy. The Public Service Act of 1904 came into effect soon thereafter. The Act provided for the Governor to appoint a Public Service Commissioner who was responsible for insuring the establishment and continuance of a proper standard of efficiency and economy in the public service sector.

The Commissioner acquired broad investigatory powers to insure compliance with the Act and make recommendations to the Governor about the general structure of public services, including the disposition of officers and offices.

Over the period, Australian public administration systems and practice developed with the blessings of the British Westminster System of Administration. In theory, Australia became a model, one of the best public administration systems in the world of developed countries.

Australia Corruption Report

Snapshot

Corruption is not an obstacle to business in Australia, which is known for its well-functioning and independent judiciary, transparent regulatory climate, and overall low level of corruption. However, corruption risks exist in relation to foreign bribery and the mining industry. The Criminal Code covers bribery of foreign and domestic public officials, while each of Australia's states and territories has its anti-corruption provisions. Public sector and private sector bribery is addressed, and both individuals and companies can be targeted.

People convicted of corruption can receive a maximum penalty of ten year long imprisonment and a fine of up to AUD 1.1 million. For a business, the penalty is a fine of up to AUD 17 million, three times the value of the received undue benefit, or 10% of the annual turnover of the company during the period in question. Australian political parties usually receive gifts and hospitality, but there is little information on gifts and hospitality in the private sector.

Judicial System

Australia's judiciary bears a low risk of corruption for companies. Bribes and irregular payments in return for favorable court decisions are very uncommon (GCR, 2015-2016). Despite this, companies report strong confidence in the independence of the judiciary (GCR, 2017-2018). Businesses are moderately satisfied with the efficiency of the legal framework pertaining to settling disputes, yet are not satisfied with its efficiency when it comes to challenging regulations (GCR, 2017-2018). The judiciary operates independently, and principles of equal treatment, procedural fairness, and judicial precedent are followed (ICS, 2017). The executive branch respects the independence of the judiciary and generally accepts its decisions rather than attempting to circumvent them (SGI, 2017).

Australia has well-established legal and court systems for litigation and arbitration. Furthermore, it is a pioneer in the development and provision of non-court dispute resolution mechanisms (ICS, 2017). Enforcing a contract in Australia takes less time than in other OECD high-income countries (DB, 2018).

Police

The risk of encountering corruption within the Australian police service is low. Surveyed business executives place high trust in the Australian police services and report few business costs of violence and crime (GCR, 2017-2018). Only five percent of Australians perceive the police as corrupt (GCB, 2017). The government has an effective mechanism in place to prevent and detect corruption in the police. Moreover, there are no reports of impunity (HRR, 2017).

A report that found that police in the state of Victoria were engaged in drug trafficking and drug use in conjunction with known traffickers, including allegations against eight officers, has been substantiated (The Guardian, Dec. 2016).

Public Services

There is a low risk of encountering corruption when acquiring public service in Australia. Companies report that irregular payments and bribes are very uncommon when obtaining public service (GCR, 2015-2016). Roughly, a sixth of Australians perceive local government officials as corrupt (GCB, 2017). About a fifth of surveyed companies reports having encountered bribery in the last five years (Deloitte, 2017). One in twenty Australian civil servants indicated in a survey that they saw a colleague acting in a corrupt manner (APSC, 2018).

Domestic and foreign companies operating in Australia enjoy great flexibility in the licensing process, given a strong rule of law that protects companies against corruption risks (ICS, 2017). Australian accounting, legal, and regulatory procedures are transparent and consistent with international standards (ICS, 2017). Starting a business takes fewer steps and less time than in any other OECD high-income country (DB, 2018). Dealing with construction permits is less time-consuming in Australia compared to other OECD high-income countries (DB, 2018).

Land Administration

Businesses are very unlikely to encounter corruption when dealing with Australia's land authorities, but there are significant risks of money laundering activity in the real estate sector. Property rights are protected by a strong rule of law (ICS, 2017). Hence, companies express strong confidence in the government's ability to protect property rights (GCR, 2017-2018). Transparency International identified significant deficiencies in Australia's rules and regulations to prevent money laundering in real estate transactions. For example, real estate agents and accountants are not covered by anti-money laundering laws and are thus, not required to follow the due diligence requirements (TI, 2017a). Registering a property takes only five days, which is much less than the OECD average of nearly 22 days (DB, 2018).

Tax Administration

There is a very low risk for companies operating in Australia to make undocumented extra payments or bribes in connection with tax payments (GCR, 2015-2016). Only five percent of Australians perceive tax officials as corrupt (GCB, 2017). Australia has tightened its anti-tax avoidance legislation, mainly affecting multinational corporations that operate in multiple tax jurisdictions (ICS, 2017). Companies spend significantly less time on paying taxes than the companies in OECD high-income countries (DB, 2018).

Adam Cranston, the son of Australia's deputy tax commissioner, Michael Cranston, was arrested for involvement in an alleged tax fraud scheme worth AUD 165 million (ABC News, May 2017). The deputy tax commissioner is not believed to have known about the conspiracy, but he faced a charge of abusing his position as a public official (ABC News, May 2017). His trial date was set for early 2019 (Financial Review, Mar. 2018).

Customs Administration

There is a moderately low risk of corruption when

dealing with the customs administration. Companies indicating irregular payments and bribes during customs procedures are very rare (GETR, 2016). Companies are satisfied with the predictability and efficiency of the clearance process (GETR, 2016). Nonetheless, companies do complain about some burdensome import procedures (GETR, 2016). It is significantly more time-consuming to comply with border procedures in Australia compared to the average among OECD high-income countries (DB, 2018).

The costs involved with border compliance are dramatically higher than those in OECD high-income countries (DB, 2018). In 2017, two border officers were accused of assisting a crime syndicate in smuggling a large amount of drugs and tobacco (ABC News, Aug. 2017). Investigations into border corruption in Australia has significantly increased in recent years, reflecting an increase in the quality of information the police have access to and an increase in capacity to assess the merit of information submitted (The West Australian, Jan. 2018).

Public Procurement

There is low risk of corruption in Australian public

procurement, but some fraud risks exist. Australia's public procurement system is generally transparent and well regulated, restricting opportunities for corrupt practices in the sector (ICS, 2017). Businesses do not report bribery as a problem during the procurement processes (GCR, 2015-2016), yet one-third of Australian companies have reported having experienced procurement fraud in the past two years (PwC, 2016). Businesses indicate that the diversion of public funds is very uncommon, and favoritism in the decisions of government officials is fairly uncommon, too (GCR, 2017-2018).

There are concerns about some tenders not being conducted transparently, particularly when *commercial-in-confidence* is cited as the reason for non-disclosure of contracts with firms in the private sector, leading to the possibility that friends of particular constituents are favored (SGI, 2017).

AusTender provides centralized publication of Australian Government business opportunities, annual procurement plans, multi-use lists, and awarded contracts. Businesses in Australia are recommended to use a specialized due diligence public procurement tool to assess potential risks.

Natural Resources

There is a moderately high risk of corruption in Australia's natural resource extraction sector. Western Australia's performance in the areas of licensing, taxation, and budgeting is poor (NRGI, 2017). Transparency International has found that the mining sectors in Western Australia and Queensland are susceptible to corruption due to weaknesses in the licensing process, including the failure to perform due diligence into companies applying for licenses (TI, 2017b).

Another concern is the *revolving door* of personnel moving between the government and the industry, as well as companies making a political contribution (TI, 2017b). The New South Wales Independent Commission Against Corruption has launched an inquiry into corruption in the grant of leases. It has already led to the resignations of multiple members of the New South Wales parliament (SGI, 2017).

In another case in 2015, the NSW Independent Commission Against Corruption accused the mining company, NuCoal, of holding exploration licenses tainted by corruption, which led to a court ruling suspending

NuCoal's licenses (Sydney Morning Herald, Sept. 2015; The Australian, Oct. 2015). Given the importance of its mining sector, Australia has started implementing the principles of the Extractive Industries Transparency Initiative (EITI) (ICS, 2017).

Legislation

Australian anti-corruption legislation is comprehensive and enforced (HRR, 2017). Anti-corruption laws are found at federal (national), state, and territory (regional) levels. At the federal level, the Criminal Code stipulates active and passive bribery of foreign and Commonwealth public officials, attempted corruption, extortion, and money laundering as criminal offenses, applying to individuals as well as companies.

Private sector bribery is primarily regulated by state and territory laws, which criminalize both active and passive bribery and, in some regions, specify false accounting-type offenses. Other relevant legislation includes the Anti-Money Laundering and Counter-Terrorism Financing Act, the Corporations Act, and the Public Service Act. Facilitation payments are not illegal in Australia, provided they are of minor value and used to obtain or expedite a *minor government action* (GLI, 2018).

Australian law does not specify which gifts are legal. However, the Australian Public Service Code of Conduct can serve as a guideline (GLI, 2018). People convicted of corruption can receive a maximum penalty of ten years and a fine of up to AUD 1.1 million (GLI 2018). For a business, the penalty is a fine of up to AUD 18 million, three times the value of the received undue benefit, or 10% of the annual turnover of the company during the period in question (GLI 2018).

Australia has ratified the United Nations Convention against Corruption (UNCAC) and the OECD Anti-Bribery Convention. However, a 2015 OECD evaluation report states that Australia needs further reforms of its foreign bribery policies and points out that current anti-corruption policy creates substantial confusion about the scope of the facilitation payments' defense.

Access to the Australian government's ComLaw for a collection of national legislation is also relevant here. As of the time of review, a new bill has been tabled, but not yet adopted, in the Australian Senate that would increase sanctions on companies and introduce corporate liability for not preventing bribery (HSF, Dec. 2017).

Civil Society

Australia's media landscape is diverse, with numerous public and private broadcasters, but ownership of private print media is highly concentrated (FotP, 2016). Australia's press environment is only considered *free* (FotP, 2017) – corporate interests notwithstanding. The government respects the rights to public assembly and freedom of speech (HRR, 2017). Civil society organizations (CSOs) operate freely, and anti-corruption bodies from all states, except for Tasmania, actively collaborate with CSOs (HRR, 2017).

The government is generally receptive to civil society organizations (SGI, 2017). However, the ingenuity of the Australian people aided by the blessings of the Westminster System always prevails. This has been a diverse history of Australia for the readers' benefit. The reason why I chose to describe it here is so you get an idea of what kind of state Australia is, how its thinking was formed, and what kind of issues I had to come across. Another reason is that it will give you a chance to decide whether or not this is the place you want to migrate to. I will further talk about the issues I faced as far as official and governmental corruption is concerned in the upcoming chapters.

What I want to stress upon is that no matter how strong the system is, it is in human nature to be corrupt and gain advantage wherever they can, particularly when they have access to undue power.

Chapter 14
The Wings of Australian Corruption

Let's start this chapter with where I left my tales of Mr. Tony Williams & Co. at New South Wales Institute of Psychiatry (the institute). Tony rarely liked my face and persona. At most, he would communicate with me through his confidante Robert Fritchley. After my refusal to change the costing as per his will, he started visibly hating and ignoring me. Of course, he did not stop exercising his *discretion* and continued instructing Jenny and Robert to use his charge rates in a way that were suitable to him in preparing tender budgets. He demonized me amongst the staff as if I was the proverbial black sheep.

Robert, who did not like to be absent from work for an extended time, was forced to take leave as his accumulated leaves were far exceeding the permissible higher limit. In his absence, I, being the second in command of the administrative position, was acting manager. I found that Tony Williams had employed three extra employees without the proper authorization from the Human Resources Department (HRD) of the New South Wales

Health Department. The modus operandi was that he would seek approval for temporary employment for an employee for three months. Later, he would renew it a couple of times. Thereafter, he would leave it as it was without a renewal. After a year or so, he would seek approval for another temporary employee without any reference to the already employed temporary employee.

When Tony was required to present the number of existing employees under his request, he showed only the permanent employees, ignoring the temporary employees who had continued getting work done without authorization. There was no system for HRD to crosscheck the number of employees. He would repeat the same tactics and continue to employ additional temporary employees without regularizing their employment.

I inquired the three employees if they had received a regular employment letter and came to know that none of them had received the employment letter/contract. This way, Tony had three employees who were working for over two years without regular authorization from the HRD. During my time working as an acting manager, I wrote to the HRD, informing them that the institute had three unauthorized employees and asked how the institute could regularize their appointment. The department took the time to respond. When Robert returned to duty, I briefed him about all the actions I had made during his absence. For most activities, he had already collected information from his confidante staff, and I only had to brief him on the action taken by me directly without involving the staff. I proudly informed him about my writing to HRD, which was about regularizing the employment of the three *temporary* employees.

He was stunned and immediately rushed to Tony. Thereafter, he informed me that I had no business to write to HRD and that he and Tony had requested HRD to withdraw my letter as it was *'sent in error.'* Surprisingly, HRD, instead of acting for the institute, accepted their request to withdraw my letter.

Thereafter, Tony and Robert started harassing me and found some fault with me every day. Robert informed those three employees that I had complained against them and thus, put their employment at risk. Both Jenny and Nicola were asked not to communicate directly with me. Robert poisoned the staff against me as if I was their enemy. Thus, they made my life miserable. I had been working there for two and a half years and had completely transformed their accounting records and reporting systems from manual to electronic. I had also streamlined the working of the administrative and support office, yet no one seemed to consider my contribution to the institute. Realizing that I had no other way to go, I lodged a complaint with ICAC against the institute. The Independent Commission Against Corruption (ICAC) has an independent statutory officer whose role and function is to hold the ICAC accountable in the way it carries out its function. The inspector's role is set out in Part 5A of the ICAC Act.

The inspector is not answerable to ICAC in any way and is located in physically separate premises from the ICAC. The inspector's role includes undertaking audits of the ICAC's operations to insure compliance with the law, dealing with complaints about the conduct of the ICAC and its current and former officers, and assessing the effectiveness and appropriateness of the ICAC's procedures.

The inspector has extensive powers to investigate the conduct of the ICAC. They have the authority to obtain documents from the ICAC and require its officers to answer their questions. The inspector can also sit as a Royal Commissioner to conduct the investigation. As a

Royal Commissioner, the inspector has extensive powers to compel witnesses to provide evidence. The inspector can deal with complaints about the conduct of the ICAC or its officers, which concern abuses of power, impropriety, misconduct of any kind, lengthy delays in investigation, and maladministration. Under the ICAC Act, maladministration is defined as action or inaction of a serious nature that is contrary to law, unreasonable, unjust, oppressive, improperly discriminatory, or based wholly or partly on improper motives.

ICAC informed me that, in the absence of evidence of taking money for a favor, the matter was not serious enough to fall under their jurisdiction and therefore, they were handing over the matter to the Auditor General of New South Wales. The office of the Auditor General informed me that the matter was under their investigation and that they would assign a senior auditor for the purpose.

Stupidly, I informed Robert about my complaint and that the Auditor General's assigned audit officer would soon visit the institute for investigation. I was informed that the Auditor General Tony Harris was a good friend and buddy of Tony Williams. The audit officer visited the institute and spent five days on the investigation, interviewing everyone important. In the end, he had a lengthy meeting with me undergoing every aspect of my complaint. He informed me that he could not find any evidence of a major irregularity and that the employment issues were not under his jurisdiction. Despite this, he advised the management to regularize the employment. He informed me that he suspected major malpractices were in practice by the complaints I made, but it appeared that they had removed all evidence, expecting the audit. He said that the audit should not have been known to them prior to his visit. My mistake of informing them stupidly gave them enough time to regularize the documentation and remove all documents in relation to major irregularities. Even the issue of the director's discretion on charge rate was beyond the jurisdiction of the auditor.

Then, within two weeks, I was informed that my position as Finance Officer was temporary and needed to be regularized. They said that with this process, the position would be advertised, and I would have to submit my application for employment, which would be considered along with other applications in a competitive process. I was asked to submit my application and was shortlisted for interviews. Robert already told about the new person likely to be selected.

As per HRD procedures, the interview committee was set up consisting of three people – two middle-level officers from the NSW Health office and Tony Williams, who chaired the committee. As expected, I was not selected. I was supposed to continue working only until the new person arrived. Tony, with the help of Robert, started troubling me for no reason. They even tried to frame sexual harassment charges against me.

Now, there was a female staff member there named Mumtaz, a young single mother of Pakistani origin. She was employed as temporary staff and worked without regularizing her employment. She assisted me with accounting matters, and as such was required to seek my approval for several accounting issues.

I had developed a good relationship with her. After my reporting against the institute, they had poisoned the minds of the staff against me. I was even prohibited from visiting the staff's common room. Instead, my assistant staff would come to my room for any instructions and reporting. One day, Mumtaz came to my room for routine work and instructions. She started questioning every instruction I gave her. I started losing my temper and began raising my voice.

Soon, Robert came, saw us arguing, and closed the door of my office while she was still inside. I mellowed my tone and she started apologizing, feeling sorry for what she was doing to me *under instructions from Robert*. We finished our meeting and she left my room. In the afternoon, Tony called me to say that there was a complaint of sexual harassment against me and that they would have to report to the police if the victim lodged an official complaint.

They pressurized Mumtaz to lodge an official complaint against me, but she hesitated. She later informed me that Robert had even threatened her, saying that she could lose her temporary job if she did not cooperate with them. She remembered all my help and training given to her patiently and sympathetically. Therefore, she did not pay any heed to their pressure.

The next day, Tony came with two security guards from the Health Department and handed me my four-week notice of termination, saying I had to leave instantly and that the security guards would take me to the Health Department's pay office situated in the nearly public hospital to get a check for the salary for the notice period. He said that he would contact me if Mumtaz filed a sexual harassment case against me.

I filed legal proceedings for unfair dismissal in the local employment tribunal. The institute hired lawyers, but I self-represented my case. Both Tony and Robert attended the tribunal hearings. After four hearings over eight weeks, the tribunal declared their decision in my favor and asked the institute to commence a conciliatory dialog with me. Tony Williams organized conciliatory hearings to resolve the dispute. The hearings took place at the HRD, New South Wales Health Department headquarters in Sydney and were attended by Tony Williams, Robert Fritchley, and one senior officer from HRD.

They organized two staff union officers to assist me. My demand was a reinstatement of my employment. They said that the position was already filled in and therefore, my demand could not be accepted. The two union officers were junior to Tony Williams. Furthermore, they appeared very weak and hesitated to question Tony Williams and the other senior HRD officer.

I was advised to accept a lump sum compensation. As I had no resources or funds to take them to court and the union officers had advised me that if I went to the court, the union would not provide any legal support, I decided to accept their offer. In Australia, any lawyer asks for an advance deposit for their fees before commencing any action. What I got was the compensation amount and a good reference letter for a future job. Thereafter, I filed a case under workers' compensation for mental stress caused by the employer. In this case, specialist injury lawyers were engaged who would take their fee from the compensation. I won this case as well. However, due to the stupidity of the lawyer handling my case, and since he was junior to the senior lawyers engaged by the Compensation Authority, I settled with a small amount of $20,000.

All of these events taught me that the one thing I needed, to escape corruption, would not be possible because it would not leave me alone. The attitude of the Australian officials was the same as those of Indian officials when it came to saving themselves and discrediting those who challenged them in the slightest manner. Sadly, this was not the last encounter I had with corrupt officials.

Chapter 15
My Destiny in Australia

After losing my employment, I started applying for a job with government agencies, as well as large and medium corporations. I must have submitted more than one thousand applications in a few months. My CV (Curriculum Vitae) was quite impressive and my name Watts was deceiving to the employers who might be taking me to be an Anglo guy.

In those days, people were quite openly racist and would rarely employ a non-white guy in an administrative or senior position. Australia had a White Australia policy until 1987, meaning only whites were invited to settle in Australia. Though this policy was abolished in 1987, people still carry the same mindset. I was invited for an interview. Upon reaching the site, I could see their shocked faces looking at me as if I was an alien from a different planet.

I would go through the long interview process. In the end, they would give me positive feedback and tell me that they would inform me if I were selected after the interview out of all other short-listed candidates. Then, I would receive a letter stating that they were sorry as my application was not successful and that they would keep my profile on their database for any future consideration. However, I never got back any response from them. This became a routine for all my interviews with government agencies. Private sector corporations would say that I was overqualified for the job or lacked adequate local experience.

I distinctly remember one incident with my application for a senior position in the Department of Finance, New South Wales Government. The person whom I was to report to chaired a selection panel of three. He came out personally to greet me as I was asked to sit waiting to be called for the interview.

He came out from the interview room excitedly – probably reading my CV and my name, Watts. I could see that all his excitement disappeared after looking at my face. He took me in and introduced me to interviewing panel of three – other two being from different departments but of a lower position in terms of seniority.

His first question was, *"What brings you here?"*

I was taken aback, sensing his sarcastic tone. I could see that the other panel members were also taken aback, staring at him.

He immediately changed his question with, *"I mean, let us know about you and why you are interested in this position?"*

He continued his sarcastic style of questioning while the other two were asking standard questions. Later, the same routine as the one I had been dealing with previously followed. I received a letter of regret, informing me that my application was unsuccessful and that my profile was retained in their database for future consideration if any suitable position arose. While applying for jobs, I was also trying the possibility of taking small contracts for accounting services. I had set up my office at my house in Castle Hill.

I would visit small businesses in the area with requests for handling their accounts. I started attending business conferences and community events. I was a regular visitor to the North Sydney ISKCON temple and soon got their accounts handling offer, partly pro bono services, and partly paid services. There, I met Peter James, a disciple of the Founder Acharya of ISKCON Srila Bhaktivedanta Swami Prabhupada. He became good friends with me, and we would regularly meet in his office and my house.

Peter introduced me to Paul Singer of Hungarian origin who was well-established in Sydney for generations. Paul was operating an accounting practice in the City of Rockdale, close to Sydney Airport, but he was not a qualified accountant. I started working from his office on a fee sharing basis. He had a good list of contacts and existing database of regular clients. His major client was Amanda Gore, an influential professional motivational public speaker.

Her clients included large corporations and the top five accounting firms like Ernst and Young (now EY), Deloitte, etc. These clients of hers would pay her over $10,000 for one lecture session of no more than half a day. I was looking after her accounts. Paul Singer pretended to her that he was supervising my work, though he did not know anything about accounting or taxation.

Soon, I realized that Paul was misguiding Amanda with his so-called ‘expert investment’ advice. She had complete faith in him and had given him full authority to control her finances. He was paying the office rent and his staff salaries from her funds. He was giving an impression to the staff and his contacts that she was his ‘girlfriend.’ I found that he had convinced her to sell her residential mansion facing the Pacific Ocean in the prestigious posh area of Cremorne and started living in a rented, sea-facing apartment in Coogee. He had convinced her to invest that money plus bank borrowing in a caravan park project Buckenderra Holiday Village in the South Coast, about 400 kilometers away from Sydney. The income from this project could not even pay the interest on bank borrowings. He was making false promises that the project would start making a profit.

When I looked at the project details and its potential, I found that the project would never be able to generate enough income, even to service the mortgage interest. The property had no potential of any capital growth as its value had fallen substantially after the purchase. Amanda was servicing the loan and other recurring expenses from her personal income.

Over a period of time, she realized that Paul had been dishonest with her and that he was siphoning her funds for his personal benefits. I was getting more popular with his clients, who knew that he was not a qualified accountant. Amanda, thinking that I was Paul's person, initially did not open with me. When she observed that I would provide my professional services independent of any input from Paul and that I would not be influenced by him while delivering my professional service, she started opening up to me and discussed issues she had with him in confidence. I encouraged her to take control of her finances independent of Paul. Paul's sister, who was aware of how her brother was a crook, was working for Amanda as her personal assistant. Amanda fully trusted her. He had appointed his sister's husband as a general manager of his accounting practice. After some time, with consent from Paul's sister, Amanda severed all relationships with Paul and prohibited him from coming to the office. Soon, the office was closed, and Amanda started her office from her apartment at Coogee. She asked me to look after accounts, taxation, and business reporting matters from her home office. I had to visit her home twice a week.

Amanda's problems were increasing. Paul took possession of Buckenderra Holiday Village telling the staff there that he was the owner. She, after consultation with her lawyers and her good friend, the managing partner of EY, decided to counter Paul's claim and take control of the property. She consulted me on how she could proceed, and we decided to go to the property. Her trusted German businessman friend, who was a self-proclaimed healer, agreed to accompany us – Amanda and me.

We drove 400 kilometers to the property, Buckenderra Holiday Village, and stayed there for a week. We learned from the staff that Paul had instructed the staff not to allow Amanda or anyone from her side to come inside of the property. It was hard for us to convince them. They had high regards for Amanda and were aware that it was she who had one hundred percent investment in the property.

The staff was typical Anglo country people, not sophisticated in their talking and behavior – called *'gronks'* in Australian slang. One of the staff members was a big built, gangster-looking, white male. With great difficulty, I established rapport with them. I needed to talk to all of them to gather information on operations, revenues, and expenses as no system was being maintained. It was being run like a small grocery shop. We set the system right and developed a new protocol for regular workings.

At the end of our trip, I advised Amanda to sell the property and get completely out of that ever-losing and nightmarish project. Her German friend advised her against selling and told her that he would manage the project for her. I asked her to consult her good friend, the managing partner of EY. After consulting him, she decided to sell off the property, as he endorsed my advice to her.

After that, Paul filed a lawsuit against Amanda claiming that he was the longstanding, unpaid manager and that he had invested his time and personal funds in managing the Buckenderra Holiday Village property. He claimed a very large amount of compensation. She involved her good friends and me in EY and Deloitte Legal. Paul lost his legal battle for the claim.

All this process of managing her affairs at a sophisticated level provided rich multi-faceted experience to my consultancy practice. My professional fees for my extended time and services generated substantial income for me in that year. After that, she told me that she would not be able to afford my services and appointed a cheap accounting professional from the country place. However, she continued to remain my friend.

Paul lodged another lawsuit claiming that he was an unpaid employee of Amanda and that he was unfairly dismissed. She required my testimony to counter his claim. I obliged her pro bono. She won the legal battle again. With that boost, my accounting and taxation practice started growing. I purchased decent-sized office premises in the heart of Sydney CBD. In 2003, I moved my office there. I faced umpteen ups and down in my professional and personal life over sixteen years, and now am holding my well-regarded consultancy business as Taxation and Business Guru. During this time, I continued studying for professional development to keep myself abreast with the ongoing changes in corporation law and ever-changing taxation legislation.

I pursued higher post-graduate studies for two years, and in 1999, I completed, with honors, a Master's degree in Administrative Law and Policy. This study helped me understand how to keep government officials honest and fair to me as well as my clients. I have had an excellent experience, without any incidence of corruption, with Australian Taxation Office and Australian Securities and Investment Commission – the two government bodies with whom I had a day-to-day interaction on behalf of my clients.

I provided my professional services to emerging community organizations. In the process, I became well-known in the communities and the Consuls General. In 2003, the then Consul General of India in Sydney Mr. Madhusudan Ganapathy was trying to bring to Australia Bharatiya Vidya Bhavan – one of largest cultural and educational organizations in the world – with headquarters situated in Bombay. All Indian governments always had and still has high regards for this organization, which was incorporated in 1938 with the blessings of Mahatma Gandhi. Its London Chapter is frequently visited by the Royal family, Prime Minister, and top ministers. For several years, Prince Charles had been an honorary patron. The British government offers healthy grants to this organization. Its New York Chapter is frequented by the current U.S.A. presidents and previous presidents.

Mr. Ganapathy approached me to help with setting up the Australian Chapter (branch) in Sydney. Until then, I was keeping away from any Indian Government official in Australia. For eleven years, I had never met the Ambassador of India to Australia or the Consuls General of

India in Australia. However, I readily accepted his request for setting up the Australian branch of Bharatiya Vidya Bhavan.

After several meetings at his office with senior Indian community leaders, we decided to incorporate a Public Company Limited by guarantee. Mr. Ganapathy requested that I do not charge any fee for twelve months. He also requested me to use my office in Sydney for his office to which I agreed for twelve months. The company was registered on 3rd July 2003, and we organized an informal launch in the Indian community on 30th July of the same year. Coincidently, India's Minister for External Affairs scheduled his visit to Australia in August 2003. Mt Ganapathy and the Indian Ambassador Mr. Rajinder Singh Rathore thought it would be a good idea to ask the Minister to launch the Australian Chapter of Bharatiya Vidya Bhavan. Mr. Ganapathy consulted me for the venue which had to be prestigious. I suggested that it should be in one of Sydney's top five-star hotels, but other community leaders wanted it in the Western suburb where the majority of Indians in Australia lived.

Mr. Ganapathy liked my idea, and we decided to have a decent launch function at the Sheraton Hotel, Sydney. I negotiated a good price with him for a large ballroom for over 300 people. He asked his Consuls to book 8-10 tables of ten seats each. However, all other Indian community leaders did not cooperate at all, as if they were boycotting. I was left alone to organize the function and fill thirty tables of ten each. Bhavan Headquarters deputed two people P A Ramakrishnan and Ash Tapase to help me organize. They sat in my office for almost six weeks.

When they observed that I was left all alone by the community leaders who were earlier appointed directors, they said to me that it was Bhavan's longstanding policy that only that person who works hard must be made the president and requested me to agree to it. They accordingly insisted that I accept the position. This further instigated all other directors. None of the Indian directors helped me. I, however, ended up with an excellent launch program in a short time of six weeks. The Consul General and the Ambassadors were delighted and since then became good friends with me. It has been sixteen years now, and I am still the president offering pro bono services, including my office premises. We have organized several larger events.

The tenure of the Ambassador and Consuls General is short for about three years. After Mr. Ganapathy, Mr. Sujan Chenoy took charge as the Consul General. He had an excellent relationship with me. During his tenure, we showcased India jointly with him and Indian tourism office all over New South Wales and South Australia. His tenure finished after three years. By then, Bharatiya Vidya Bhavan was well-known all-over Australia and was being considered by the Australian government organizations like the Indian Cultural Ambassador and would be approached for any information on India. After Mr. Chenoy, Mr. Amit Dasgupta took charge. He was initially quite nice to me and praised my achievements a lot. He asked me for my projects where he could help me. I gave him a brief of two of my lengthiest standing projects for which I was fighting with the government authorities:

- Installing the statue of Mahatma Gandhi in Sydney CBD. For the past four years, I had been working on it with the Lord Mayor of the City of Sydney and other authorities. I had collected support letters from several organizations, including one from the director of Sydney Peace Foundation, which was greatly patronized by the Lord Mayor.

- New South Wales Premier's Award for Indian Community. My fight with the State government had been on for three years. During my tenure as a Commissioner of Community Relations Commission for New South Wales, I found that the government had been hosting annual community awards for the Chinese community. I raised an idea of similar awards for Indian community, which they laughed away. I then had to start my fight with the government that instigated the government. As a result, my tenure as a commissioner was not renewed.

Mr. Amit Dasgupta happily took these projects from me, promising that he would intervene and use his authority to exert pressure. However, I soon found that he, after taking the projects from me, had completely cut me off. He did not do anything for my project for Gandhi's statue in Sydney CBD. His daughter was studying at the University of New South Wales. He made a deal with the university that they install a bust of Mahatma Gandhi in the university and he would get them popular treatment from the Indian government for international students.

After eighteen months or so, the university installed the bust. Mr. Dasgupta was asked to help them with the inaugural function and then annual features on 2nd October (Gandhi's birthday anniversary) and around 30th January (Gandhi's martyrdom day anniversary). In this, he totally ignored Bharatiya Vidya Bhavan and me and instead assigned the responsibility for the two functions to his favorite lady from the Indian community. Two years after giving him details of my second project, the New South Wales Premier, Ms. Christina Kennelly agreed to commence Indian Community Awards.

Again, Dasgupta completely ignored me and Bharatiya Vidya Bhavan Australia, giving all credit to another one of his own community's members. He could not tolerate the popularity of Bharatiya Vidya Bhavan with the government organizations and tried to undermine Bhavan and me in every way he could by abusing his authority. He even tried to break my influence and create a rift between the board members of Bhavan and me by ignoring me and addressing the directors individually. When I objected to him bypassing my president's position, he became like my enemy speaking against me in the community.

He reminded me of my father's saying, *"Power*

corrupts, and absolute power corrupts absolutely."

Mr. Dasgupta soon retired but left sore notes against me for his successor. The Indian Ambassador, to whom all the Indian Counsels General (from each city) reported at that time, was Mrs. Sujatha Singh. Amit Dasgupta did not feel comfortable with working under a female boss. He told me that he and Sujatha Singh were of the same seniority and that she was promoted due to 'political influence.' He openly tried to undermine her authority. However, I found her very fair, just, and completely clean.

I had taken up my fight with SBS (Special Broadcasting Services) TV – a government-owned and operated entity – to broadcast Hindi news. It broadcast news in most of the world's major languages, but Hindi was not included. SBS first said that Hindi speaking people in Australia were not an insignificant number. I then provided detailed statistics with extensive analysis of the number of Hindi speaking people in comparison with various other ethnicities for whom they were broadcasting in their respective languages.

They then they came up with the excuse that there were technical problems of sharing the news with India. I took up the matter with the Ambassador Sujatha Singh. She spoke with them and understood their technical issue. She organized an alternative source of Hindi news from India, and SBS agreed to start broadcasting Hindi news from India. They organized a launch event, in which she was the chief guest. Amit Dasgupta and I were invited, too.

In her opening speech, Mrs. Sujatha Singh acknowledged my contribution. Amit did not like this at all and later said to me that she did a special favor to me. She liked my work and respected me a lot. Amit Dasgupta was furious at this and even tried to malign her by saying she was attracted to me and we might be having an affair. He was even spreading rumors about my 'illegal taxation practice,' and that I could soon be in 'big trouble from the Australian Tax Office.' Nothing could deter my spirit. People at Bhavan headquarters always liked and supported me, and I continued to be the organization's president. In addition, I established another organization dedicated to Mahatma Gandhi, called the International Center for Nonviolence Australia. Dr. Ela Gandhi (granddaughter of Mahatma Gandhi) based in Durban South Africa graced me by accepting my invitation to launch this center at the premises of New South Wales Parliament House in February 2013.

In Australia, property buying is a passion, and there are substantial taxation incentives for those investing in properties. Banks are liberal in financing the purchase of these properties. Property value increases significantly every year, and one can use the additional equity generated to buy further properties. Over the ten years of my consultancy practice, I, with my wife Bhoji, ended up owning ten properties. Then, due to my argument with one bank officer's corrupt and intimidating behavior and unethical legal professionals, I lost all the properties, one by one, by 2007. I continued my legal battle against the bank, but ultimately, lost it. In 2010, Bhoji and I were declared bankrupt. However, with my prolonged argument with the Taxation Professional Board, I could retain my taxation practicing licenses and other professional licenses and thus continued my consultancy practice diligently.

I refused to give up and continued to work for the betterment of my family. What I realized was that trying to fight corruption was a useless cause because it was getting me literally nowhere, and somehow was always in one kind of fix or the other. It was like there was no way I could try to be a businessman and yet retain good, incorruptible stance on life.

Chapter 16
Inescapable Corruption

In both countries, even though I had friends at high designations, it was impossible to get work done without some kind of bribery. Corruption had crept into the administrative systems and made it impossible for anyone to succeed. I believe that *corruption* is the most powerful enemy of human rights.

Definition of Corruption (Merriam Webster Dictionary)

1a: *Dishonest or illegal behavior especially by powerful people (such as government officials or police officers): DEPRAVITY*

1b: *Inducement to wrong by improper or unlawful means (such as bribery) the corruption of government officials.*

The language of corruption is universal. It has no caste, no religion, no color, and is blind. That is another thing I learned from my experiences. Corruption affects us all. It threatens sustainable economic development, ethical values, and justice. It destabilizes our society and endangers the rule of law. Delays in infrastructure development, poor building quality, and layers of additional costs are all consequences of corruption. Forms of corruption vary and include bribery, extortion, cronyism, nepotism, parochialism, patronage, influence peddling, graft, and embezzlement. The entire society is affected as a result of the inefficient allocation of resources, the presence of a shadow economy, and low-quality education and healthcare.

In this book so far, I have described only some of the corruption examples that I experienced personally and which affected me adversely. Let us now look at the domain of corruption in general of both countries.

Indian Corruption

A few months ago, a survey revealed that Asia's most corrupt country is India. The bane of corruption runs deep here. It is permeated into every institution, every social program, and every strand of the country's nervous system. It is not only me saying this, but there are also cold, hard facts and statistics supporting each of these claims. Current statistics indicate that 54% of India's population has paid a bribe when accessing public services and institutions. Here are a few other numbers about the discredited state of affairs in India.

38% Of Land And Property Deals In India Involve Bribes

In India, 38% of land deals involve some form of bribes, mostly because for the buyer, that is the only option. The entire nexus of government officials, politicians, judicial officers, real estate developers, and law enforcement officials control the property trade, wherein they acquire and sell land illegally. These groups remain well protected and are highly connected, for the most part, making it almost impossible to renege on a deal.

62% Of Law Enforcement Officers Take A Bribe

The police collect the highest number of bribes. Passport verifications make up 30% of the average bribe paid by a regular Indian in a year, while traffic violations make up 25%. The methods are numerous, and the amounts are far-reaching, ranging from botched breath-analyzer tests charging rupees 2500 to 500 for passport verification.

60% Of Road Stops For Truckers Are For Extorting Money

According to Transparency International, truckers pay rupees 2220 million in bribes every year. Authorities such as government regulators, police, forest and sales, excise force stoppages on roads, and 60% of these are for extorting money. These delays lead to an egregious loss in productivity.

60% Of People Who Got Their Driving License From An Agent Haven't Taken The Driving Exam

The procedure to get a driving license in India is highly askew, with research showing that it is possible for people with little to no ability to get a license through the use of agents. A study showed that agents helping unqualified drivers obtain licenses and bypass the legally required driving examination was a widespread practice. Among those surveyed, around 60% of the license holders had not even taken the licensing exam, and 54% of those license holders had failed an independent driving test.

31% Of Members Of Parliament Have Criminal Cases Against Them

Political parties are the most corrupt institutions in India. They have a corruption rate of 4.4 on a scale of 5 (1 being least corrupt and 5 being highest). In 2012, criminal cases were pending against 31 percent of members of parliament and the legislative assembly. The dismal state of affairs has led to a lot of political candidates promoting their criminality as an indication of their ability to defend the interests of their communities.

Petty corruption in 11 basic services

The monetary value of petty corruption in eleven basic services, such as education, healthcare, and the judiciary amounts to about Rupees 3,19,72,50,00,000 annually.

India's Telecom Ministry Siphoned Approximately $30 Billion

The 2G spectrum scam, which saw licenses granted to mobile phone companies during an irregular sale, cost the government (well at least those who weren't part of the deal) rupees 1.76 trillion.

Just About 40% Of Grain Intended For The Poor Reaches Them

A report by the World Bank showed that only 40% of grain handed out to the poor reaches its target. This report says that the aid programs in India are beset by corruption, bad administration, and underpayments. As recent as today February 2019, the Indian government's various health programs are operated by the government-appointed staff to administer free medicines for chronic and problematic diseases like tuberculosis. There is no proper clean supervision of these government staff members. Their job is to administer/supply lifesaving medicines free of cost.

They tell the patients, even in severe and advanced stages of the disease, that these medicines are very pricy which they are getting for free and thus saving them large money. Therefore, they must share their benefit with these government servants and pay them cash before getting the medicines. If the patient refuses, then no medicine is given, citing some lame excuses.

Australian Corruption

Australian culture has developed through some strange phenomena involving total disrespect to human rights and gross inequity. Until 1901, women had no voting rights. As recently as 1965, the aboriginal people were still considered Flora and Fauna and were not included in the population for any policy. Until 1987, Australia strictly practiced its policy of Whites Only. Even today in 2019, Australia has no Bill of Rights.

Naturally, the advanced economy of Australia is rife with corruption in every field. Let us look at some key areas which directly affect the common man.

Public Sector Corruption

Public sector corruption refers to the misuse of public power or position with an expectation of undue private gain or advantage for self or others. It may include:

- Bribery
- Embezzlement
- Fraud
- Extortion
- Trading in influence

- Perverting the course of justice
- Exchanging goods for money or information

Corrupt conduct can occur directly through the improper or unlawful actions of public sector officials or through the actions of individuals operating in the private sector who attempt to influence the functions of government inappropriately. Organized crime groups try to corrupt public officials to gain access to public funds, information, protection, and other services to facilitate criminal activities. These officials are likely to be from law enforcement agencies, border agencies, and agencies that issue identification documents.

Corruption has a severe impact on government, industry, and national security. It prejudices the rule of law and distorts markets. It can inhibit foreign investment and international credit ratings and damages Australia's reputation as a safe, reliable economy in which to invest and trade. It can also harm cooperation and relationship with foreign governments and law enforcement agencies.

Corruption of public sector officials has substantial multiplier effects and benefits for organized crime. There may be important links between corruption in the public sector and organized crime groups that, by their very nature, remain hidden. The key challenge in identifying and investigating corruption is that corrupt conduct occurs in secret between consenting parties who are frequently skilled at deception.

Corruption in Australian Sport

While a diversity of sports is played in Australia, the predominant codes are, at levels of participation and public interest – Australian Rules Football, rugby league, rugby union, soccer (or 'football'), cricket, netball, swimming, tennis, motorsports, cycling and the 'races' – thoroughbred, harness, and greyhound racing. Almost all of the listed sporting codes have been the subject of controversy in the 2009–13 period considered here and most of these have been affected by allegations of corruption.

The following synopsis describes a select group of substantiated or (currently) alleged cases of corruption and otherwise unethical behavior affecting Australian sport in the five years from 1st January 2009 to 31st December 2013. These do not represent the full range of cases, in volume or manifestation that occur during this period, but were purposefully selected to:

- Demonstrate some of the more serious cases of

corruption affecting Australian sports.

- Illustrate the spectrum of behavior characterizing these incidents and the sports they affected.
- Highlight where corruption could be described as entrenched in specific Australian sporting codes and industries.

The cases are categorized according to Gorse and Chadwick's (2011) classification, with the qualification that not all cases are an exact fit and potentially encapsulate different facets of corruption, specifically match-fixing and doping.

Match-Fixing (Betting Related)

Soccer

Victorian Premier League (Southern Stars FC)

The most prominent case of match-fixing in Australia to date was reported in September 2013 and involved players and staff engaged with the Southern Stars FC, a football club in the second-tier Victorian Premier League. Sportradar, the internet betting integrity monitoring agent, detected irregular betting patterns associated with at least five Southern Stars games, which were characterized by 'unusually poor play' by some of the players (six charged over soccer match-fixing scandal). Victoria Police subsequently charged six people with match-fixing offenses, including the coach, four players (all of whom were from the United Kingdom) and a Malaysian national.

The latter acted as a liaison between the coach and players and a betting syndicate based in Hungary and Malaysia. The syndicate is reported to have made an estimated $2m on the five thrown games played between 21st July and 13th September 2013.

On 25th October 2013, the Football Federation of Australia (FFA) suspended the coach and four players for breach of the FFA's National Code of Conduct (Southern Stars players and coach) banned by FFA following criminal charges for alleged match-fixing (ABC News Online, 25 October).

The four players all subsequently pleaded guilty to three or four match-fixing charges and were convicted and fined between $1,200 and $3,000 each (footballer rigged matches because of 'slave-like existence,' court hears).

Rugby League

National Rugby League (Ryan Tandy and others)

Ryan Tandy, a player in the National Rugby League (NRL) team the Canterbury Bulldogs, was found guilty in October 2011 of *'dishonestly obtaining a financial advantage by deception'* through spot-fixing an August 2010 game between Canterbury and the North Queensland Cowboys. The fix referred to a play Tandy made early into the game with the intention of awarding a potential penalty to the Cowboys (Davies, 2011). The TAB detected a 'betting plunge' on the game, where 95 percent of bets placed were on the first scoring play to be a penalty goal from the Cowboys. Tandy was fined $4,000 and put on a twelve month good behavior bond (Prichard, 2012). He was later dismissed from the Bulldogs.

Match-Fixing (Non-Betting Related)

Australian Rules football

Australian Football League (Melbourne Football Club)

The Australia Football League's (AFL) Integrity Unit investigated the Melbourne Demons in 2012 about allegations of deliberately losing games (i.e. 'tanking') in the 2009 football season. The allegations first surfaced during an interview with an ex-player (and supported by other personnel) that one of the officials eventually sanctioned by the AFL had suggested during a club meeting of the '*perils of winning more than four games that year'* (Wilson, 2013: np). It was suspected that tanking was proposed to promote the Demons chances of receiving priority in the following year's draft pick (Wilson, 2012).

Clubs that win less than five games in a season are eligible for priority draft pick. The allegations emerged from statements made by club officials and players suggesting matches were being played in a way to insure any loss (Wilson, 2012).

While the investigation concluded there was no evidence of any tanking having occurred or of management directing players to tank, the AFL found the coach and the general manager of football operations guilty of '*acting in a manner prejudicial to the interests of the competition'* (AFL, 2013a).

The little context was given in the final report from the AFL as to what this act constituted but was presumed by the media to allude to the alleged statements made at the club meeting by the two officials investigated (Wilson, 2013). Both were suspended, and the club was fined a total of $500,000. The club's general manager was relieved of his duties as manager of club development in October, 2013.

Risks to Australian Sport

Some risk factors are identified as increasing the opportunity for corruption in sport. These include:

- The 'closed environment' in which athletes and sporting officials operate
- Differential responses to what is perceived as illegal
- Negligible pay and lack of financial security, particularly among second and lower-tier players and officials
- The link between sport and making money; crucially, the increased options available for betting and wagering (e.g., betting on defeats, specific plays) and the ascendancy of online gambling.

Protections in Place

The sustained international focus on corruption in sport, combined with a reassessment of risks to Australian sport, has seen the introduction of a range of protections by both government and national sporting bodies. These comprise the following:

- Endorsement of national policies on match-fixing and sports doping
- Establishment of sport integrity units both at the national level and by individual sporting codes
- The inclusion of specialist intelligence units in law enforcement agencies; and
- Creation of relevant criminal offenses in state and territory legislation.

Corruption Rife in International Student Sector of Leading Australian Universities

Australia's leading universities, including the prestigious University of Sydney and the Australian National University, have engaged corrupt education agents who are falsifying the academic records of prospective international students to ensure their acceptance into the Australian tertiary system, according to an investigation by ABC TV's Four Corners.

A Four Corners investigation reveals that soft-marking, mass-cheating, and the bribery of academics are commonplace in Australian universities.

Authorities Accused Of Targeting

Suspected Fleeing Saudi Women

The program, which exposed soft-marking, mass-cheating, and the bribery of academics as a commonplace occurrence in Australia's higher education sector, reinforces concerns that Australia's booming international student market is contributing to a decline in academic standards through the routine acceptance of students with inadequate English proficiency. The investigation found many students were arriving at Australian universities with scores of 4.5 on the International English Language Testing System – an international standardized test of English language proficiency - well below the test's recommended minimum score of 7 for university entry.

Almost one in three new graduates are still looking for work four months after finishing their studies. The revelations come as the state's most prestigious universities grapple with the fallout of the Herald's investigation into systematic cheating, which revealed that up to 1,000 students hired a Sydney-based company to write their assignments and sit online tests.

Pressure on the state's tertiary sector also intensified last week after the NSW's Independent Commission Against Corruption published findings that the reliance upon revenues from international students were creating conditions 'conducive to corruption' inside universities.

"Every single university we spoke to has said that at some point they've had problems with some of their agents with false documentation and often collusion with their students," ICAC's Robert Waldersee said.

A number of Chinese education agents, who represent the University of Sydney, the University of Technology, Sydney, and the University of Newcastle, were found by the ABC to be willing to accept forged academic transcripts with the network of collusion extending into the universities' internal processes.

"In some cases, the universities have hired independent verifiers to check documents and qualifications only to find that the students and the agents have been colluding or bribing the document verifiers as well," Mr. Waldersee said.

He. Waldersee said the ICAC had been informed of another case where university managers had a personal and financial relationship with the agents they were supposed to be overseeing. The mass enrolment of students with inadequate English skills has contributed to a symbiotic culture of cheating and bribery among students and wilful blindness by the university administrations.

University of Sydney academic Zena O'Connor, whose elective course in the university's architecture faculty nets the university between $250,000 and $450,000, told the ABC the income stream from international students was *huge*.

A direct consequence of this, she said, was a, *"level of extreme plagiarism that I didn't see five or ten years ago,"* accompanied by *"an unwritten rule not to fail students."*

"Often their emails and essays are almost impossible to decipher," she said. "And some of these students are at the end of their degrees. It's horrifying."

Ms. O'Connor's claims came one week after the University of Sydney vice-chancellor Michael Spence announced he would personally chair a university-wide task force on academic misconduct, following revelations by the Herald that the university might have failed to detect dozens of instances of cheating across its faculties. The passing of students with abysmal English is already linked to egregious consequences once these students enter the job market.

In 2009, Bhavesh Shah, a graduate nurse from the University of Western Sydney, mistakenly fed an elderly patient a cup of dishwashing liquid because he had been unable to read the label. Shah, who has since been struck off the register, failed the English language test six times after he became a registered nurse.

Corrupt legal system only benefits lawyers and rich criminals

In an Independent Australia exclusive, five-time Walkley Award-winning journalist Evan Whitton explains why the legal system is fabulous for lawyers and rich criminals. Taxpayers pay the wages of judges, police, prosecutors, legal aid lawyers, etc. They are entitled to know that a truth-seeking system, as in France, costs less and delivers more justice than the adversary system which England bequeathed to its colonies, i.e., Ireland, India, the U.S., Australia.

In the adversary system, lawyers question witnesses, and, at $10+ a minute, have an incentive to spin the process out. Trials can take months. Untrained judges do the decent thing that they try to stay awake.

Justice Russell Fox researched the law for eleven years after he retired from the Federal Court. He concluded that justice means fairness to everyone, including victims and taxpayers, requires a search for the truth; truth means reality, and the search for truth gives a system its morality. Otherwise, the winner is likely to be the one with more money and cleverer lawyers. The adversary system does not seek the truth, and hence fails all Justice Fox's tests: it is unfair, unreal, immoral, and unjust.

In France, the evidence is not concealed, and judges do not let lawyers pollute the truth with sophistry, i.e., false insinuations, false statements, invalid arguments, etc. 95% of guilty defendants are convicted. The innocent are rarely charged. In the adversary system, six rules which conceal significant evidence from jurors make it difficult to charge, let alone convict, serial rapists, and white collar criminals, e.g., tax evaders, inside traders, price-fixers.

The rules and defense lawyers' sophistry get more than 50% of guilty defendants off, but at least 1% of people in prison are innocent. On the civil side, the negligence law is unfair to doctors and industrialists. Libel law outside the

U.S. is unfair to citizens. It makes it difficult to report how they are being done down by rogues.

Judge Russell Fox says the public knows that *"Justice marches with the truth."*

Informed taxpayers thus support a change to a truth-seeking system. Six times as many (trained) judges (and fewer lawyers) are required, yet it is cheaper.

Any parrot-house of sophistry deployed to resist the change can be safely ignored. Lawyers are 0.02% of the population.

Corruption in Construction

As allegations of corruption in Australia's construction unions continue to emerge, the scandal – purportedly involving underworld heavyweight Mick Gatto and bikie gangs – appears to be an underbelly script waiting to happen.

Union official Dave Noonan discussed the corruption scandal in terms of the industry's *"rotten apples."* This is a dangerous analogy to use. Not only does it suggest that successful reform lies in picking out the few corrupt officials, but it also fails to address how and why corruption has taken root.

With widespread allegations of corruption within the building unions involving accepted practices of extortion, death threats, and collusion with organized crime, it is the systems and practices that have allowed this conduct to occur and continue – the rotten barrel – that must be addressed, not the rotten apples.

Increasingly, however, media reports of corruption in the building industry are being framed in terms of how it can be fixed. Much attention has been given to the royal commission versus taskforce debate. Both sides have their merits. Taskforces are generally cheaper and less time-consuming whereas royal commissions are usually granted greater scope and investigative powers. Focusing on how to fix the rotten barrel is both a positive and practical way of approaching the issue. The risk in taking this approach is that the issue becomes politicized. Scrutiny of the causes and the true nature of corruption in the building industry risks being reduced in favor of focusing on the political role of unions.

In closing, it is strange that in Australia the senior ministers in the government like the State Premier (equivalent to the rank of State Governor in the USA) can resign and 'retire from politics' and immediately get a high profile and highly remunerative ongoing consultancy position or assignment in a large private corporation. Their main role is handling government affairs. In other words, even though they are supposedly out of the government, they are still the ones controlling all the things that are in power or have any kind of significant impact.

What a Height of Corruption!

I still marvel at how low people can fall to accomplish their means. For them, corruption or bribery is of no concern or problem. It is their daily job and right without any thoughts of immorality. People from the lowest to the highest strata of society are liable to corruption. The higher in the position they are, the more corrupt they will turn out to me. In the end, I would like to say that it is not 'places' that are corrupt, or even governments. It is the people who make them. Therefore, there is a need for a change in mindset and training.

People, particularly those in power, should be taught to use it responsibly and not abuse it at any cost, for personal gains. Of course, this will only happen in due time, but now is the moment to start. Education people on human rights needs to be started at an early age, right from primary school, and continue up to every class every year, including at the university level.

www.ingramcontent.com/pod-product-compliance
Lightning Source LLC
Chambersburg PA
CBHW021219090426
42740CB00006B/281

* 9 7 8 1 9 5 0 0 8 8 3 1 7 *